What Is That Boy Going To Do Next?

What Is That Boy Going To Do Next?

✦

A Memoir

George Hemingway Isom

iUniverse, Inc.
New York Lincoln Shanghai

What Is That Boy Going To Do Next?
A Memoir

Copyright © 2005 by George Hemingway Isom

iUniverse books may be ordered through booksellers or by contacting:

iUniverse
2021 Pine Lake Road, Suite 100
Lincoln, NE 68512
www.iuniverse.com
1-800-Authors (1-800-288-4677)

ISBN: 0-595-33804-6

Printed in the United States of America

To James, Joseph, and Ben Jr.
and in memory of Mama, Babe and the Ole Man

Two roads diverged in a wood, and I—
I took the one less traveled by,
And that has made all the difference.

Robert Frost

Contents

Acknowledgments

I would like to thank Harry "Swede" Lagerstedt, who also served on the Andy, for jogging my memory more than once. Thanks to J. Gayle Camarda, Noel C. Holobeck, and Kathleen Smith of the St. Louis Public Library and Jane Spence of the St. Joseph County Public Library (situated in South Bend) for their able assistance. I am also grateful to Ms. Wood, the chimesmaster at the University of Illinois in Champaign, for helping me revive the memory of my bus stop in Champaign. Finally, many, many thanks go to my wife Jeanne who not only put up with a self absorbed husband for months but tirelessly read the manuscript and contributed thoughtful commentary and suggestions.

Preface

"Why are you so different" and "Why can't you be like so and so" are questions asked of teenagers of every generation. I was a teenager regarded as "different" and was asked those questions too. Teenagers are seen as different for a variety of reasons, depending upon the viewer. In my case, it was because I was a nonconformist. Many people believe being different is a harbinger of a life of gloom and doom. To that, I emphatically say—"it ain't necessarily so."

Moreover, I believe teenagers perceived as different should nevertheless be who they are—and honorably do their own thing. Seek approval and acceptance but not at the cost of personal integrity is my advice to teenagers concerned about being different.

To parents, teachers and others, I say teenagers should be respected for their differences as well as for their ability to conform.

As for me, I happily did my own thing virtually throughout my teens. And the aim of this book is to show that this was a rich and productive seven year period.

1

Mound City

In June, 1945, despite my actions to keep it from happening, I graduated from grade school. Like an interminable stay in the hospital, school was a real drag. And I tried to erase it from my consciousness by seeking a variety of new and different experiences elsewhere—sometimes with my parents' approval.

When the school year started in September, 1944, as an 8th. grader in the final year of grade school, I was expected to be excited about returning to school and looking forward to graduation. But that was not the case with me as I hauled myself off to Waring School on opening day.

After a few weeks, I couldn't take it any more and started playing hooky. Since Babe and the Ole Man left for work before James and I got up, and James left for school ahead of me, it was easy for me to stay home secretly. In the beginning, it was a matter of conscience, and I felt guilty about not going to school. The Ole Man and Babe not only expected me to go but demanded that I go. But as the number of hooky-playing days added up, instead of feeling guilt, I felt relief.

Often when playing hooky, I stayed home and listened to radio programs. Kate Smith, of the *Kate Smith Show*, was a wonderful singer who could arouse the deepest feelings of patriotism with her rendition of "God Bless America." But the thing I liked best about her program was listening to her announcer, Ted Collins, open each show with his booming voice crying out, "It's high noon in New York!" Those words had the magic of "Open, Sesame!," conjuring up thrilling images of faraway places and exciting my curiosity. Each time I heard them, I was encouraged to believe there was a marvelous world out there somewhere beyond the borders of Mill Creek and St. Louis.

In spite of the radio programs and movies that disparaged colored folk, I was a big fan of both media, for they excited my imagination and stimulated my desire to know things. Many movies, for example, passed on the idea that white people were superior to Negroes in every meaningful way—intelligence, talent, morality, physical appearance, civility, and even hygiene. But I saw a few that were an

1

exception to the belittling rule. One such movie was *Casablanca* which starred Humphrey Bogart and Ingrid Bergman. In this movie set in Africa—the first I ever saw that was not about exotic animals, white hunters or a white guy talking to a monkey and swinging through the trees—a black guy had a great job singing and playing the piano in a nightclub. My attention was riveted on this character named Sam, played by Dooley Wilson. He was a source of pride, and I prized every scene that included him.

Popular radio programs like *Jack Armstrong: The All American Boy*—who was white—sent out the same message of white superiority. I didn't buy into any of it because I was pretty sure of myself and believed I could cut it as well as or better than any kid my age—white, black or whatever.

Some afternoons when I didn't go to school, I'd drop by the barbershop. The best checker games in town took place there as well as much thought-provoking discussion on race issues and the workings of Jim Crow. Mr. Jones, a barber and deacon in church, came straight out and said, "Crackers don't like niggers and think they're better than us. And there ain't nothin we can do to change that. So I say stay way from 'em." One time I told him about a white girl on the streetcar who stared me in the face and winked. She was clearly flirting, and I wanted to say something to her. But I didn't. He said, "Boy, you were right to stay in your place." I didn't like the way he put it, but I understood his meaning. The other barber, who fancied himself to be a proper English speaker, wasn't as blunt as Mr. Jones and was fond of saying, "I believe Negroes have to be a credit to the race." After mulling it over, I guessed he meant black folk should do only good deeds because a bad deed by a single colored person would make the entire race look bad. I couldn't put my finger on it, but I thought there was something wrong with that thinking.

Nobody ever sat me down and explained the ABC's of Jim Crow or told me why white folk and black folk didn't mix. Black and white people seemed comfortable with segregation, regarding it as though it was the natural order of things like night and day or winter, spring, summer and fall. There was nothing to question about it. But my imagination told me this was not natural. What's going on? I wondered.

The school year had been underway for a month when I felt the need to do something special, to get into something real interesting. Yet I was pretty cool and didn't rush into anything, remembering a lesson learned when I was 9. At that time, numbed by boredom and desparate to do something different, I tried to smoke cigarettes and thought a great way to do it was to roll my own. So I would search for cigarette butts on the sidewalks, select the longest ones, split them open and collect the tobacco from them. Then, from the mixture of all the tobacco collected, I'd spread tobacco into strips of paper from brown-paper bags and roll them into cigarettes as the cowboys did in my beloved western movies. To my chagrin, this solution to the doldrums turned out to be a misadventure, causing me to end up in Homer G. Phillips Hospital with diptheria.

In October, I was depressed and had to do something exciting. Playing hooky, listening to the radio and other things were no longer working. So I found a job as a delivery boy, in the late afternoon, at Ed's Drugstore. There, I had personal contact with white people for the first time. Before then, they were merely faces I saw when taking a ride on a streecar. In the beginning, neither I nor white kids acknowledged each others presence—no nods, smiles, or hellos. Only cold stares and silence. But as I rode my bicycle in their neighborhood making deliveries, a few boys began to give me a friendly hello. After a short while, I'd hang out for a few minutes, listening to them carrying on about baseball.

One afternoon after the 1944 World Series in St. Louis between the Cardinals and Browns ended, I ran into some white kids gabbing animatedly about the star players of each team. One boy said the Cardinals won because they had the best players, naming Stan Musial, Marty Marion and Harry Brecheen as examples. Another boy insisted that the Browns should have won because of stars like Jack Kramer, George Sisler and Vern Stephen. On the sideline, I listened to their impassionate opinions about white ball players and wanted to tell them about some great black players like Satchel Paige, Hilton Smith, Josh Gibson and James Cool Papa Bell.

These players, and others like them in the Negro League, were just as good or better than the white players they mentioned. I kept up with them through the weekly black newspaper, the *Argus*, and heard black kids and other people at the barbershop rave about them. They also stood out in the black-all-star East-West Game played at Comiskey Park in Chicago every year. It was most unlikely that these kids had heard of these colored players because the white media didn't cover them much. And since they showed little or no interest in what I had to say about anything, I kept this information and my opinion to myself.

Disregarding the lack of real dialogue between them and me, I still wanted to know about their world. As I intently listened to them with interest, I became aware of differences among them and realized that they didn't see themselves as merely white people but as Jews, Germans, Italians, Irish or Poles. That was news to me. And so was the discovery that some members of their families didn't speak English at home but a different language. One kid whose family came from Germany told me—to my surprise—that I was speaking German each time I asked for my favorite lunchmeat, Braunschweiger, at the grocery store. It was fascinating to learn that within their various households there were different religious beliefs, different language newspapers, foods, music, and dances. Consequently, I began to see them as people of diverse cultural antecedents with some sort of identification with the country of their forebears.

In November, 1944 a highly publicized movie called *Meet Me In St. Louis* made its debut at the Lowe's State Theater in St. Louis. It was the subject of joyous conversation at the drugstore. White kids came in whistling and singing some of the songs from the movie. As a resident of St. Louis who hadn't seen the movie because it opened in a white theater and hadn't yet made its way to a black one, I felt embarrassed and excluded. Yet white kids tantalizingly carried on about the movie as if I was not in their presence. Seemingly, they were oblivious of the segregation practices that prevented me from seeing the movie on an equal footing with them. Though I couldn't expect any one of them to say, "Excuse us for carrying on in this way in your presence," it would have helped to believe they thought it unfair that I was denied the right to see the movie as early as they—and in the same theater.

Colored folk lived near Ed's Drugstore, but since it was in a white neighborhood, the customers were virtually all white. Eddie, the Jewish owner of the drugstore, was a single young guy and the first white man whom I got to know anything about close up. I liked him right away for his friendly, easy-going manner. He was fun and liked to kid around in an acceptable way, unlike those white men who rubbed their hand over colored kids head while pretending to be friendly but curiously hoping it would bring them good luck. Popular among such people was the saying, "Rub a nigger's head for good luck." Not once did Eddie do or say anything demeaning. He was hip, smart and a real nice guy. I once asked him if he'd ever heard of Satchel Paige, and to my surprise, he had not only heard of him but of Cool Papa Bell and Josh Gibson as well.

Bill, Eddie's full-time clerk, made sales and rang up money in the cash register. To me that was the coolest job in the world. He started about 2 in the afternoon and worked until 9 at night. Occasionally he failed to show up, and I helped out when there were no deliveries to be made. I quickly learned where various merchandise was, and when a customer asked for something I couldn't find, I'd ask Eddie where to find it. One day, without prior notice, Bill quit, and Eddie had to hire another clerk. I immediately asked Eddie for the job, reminding him that I knew how to do it. But I didn't really expect him to give it to me. Black drugstore clerks in a white neighborhood were unheard of in St. Louis. Eddie said

I could have it temporarily while he looked for somebody else. My age didn't come up because I'd already told him I was 17, within the legal dropout age.

I was so happy! I had to share the feeling with somebody. But because I had to quit school entirely in order to start work at 2, I couldn't tell Babe or the Ole Man, for there was no way either one would approve of it. And since I didn't have any close buddies, there was only James to share it with. Beaming, one morning in November before James left for school, I said, "Eddie's clerk quit and I got the job—at least for the time being."

"What time do you start work?" he asked, with indifference.

"I start at 2 and finish at 9."

"Then you intend to quit school?" he asked.

"I'll have to—to start at 2."

"I just hope you know what you're doing."

I didn't expect him to react with enthusiasm, but at least I told somebody. He said he wouldn't tell Babe or the Ole Man, after I told him to keep it a secret.

Soon Eddie stopped looking for somebody else to replace Bill and made me his regular clerk. I was beside myself with joy, ringing up sales, making change and carrying on with a full-time job. I figured I had it made as long as I stayed a few steps ahead of the truant officer. And to do that, I only had to continue intercepting his notices to the Ole Man.

At times when business was slow, Eddie and the haberdasher next door would stand around in front of their stores and talk about various things. The haberdasher, Mr. Goldenberg, was much older than Eddie and did most of the talking. He used to say to Eddie, "The most important thing for a person to have is confidence." I wondered what he meant but never figured it out. I enjoyed eavesdropping on their conversations and did so whenever I could. They talked a lot about the war in Europe, giving me an opportunity to see it through their eyes.

2

To No Avail

For several weeks, I had a great time clerking and hoped it would never end. I kept the truant officer at bay, and Babe and the Ole Man weren't any wiser, thinking I was only working after school. One day, while I was on a stepladder reaching upward to stock some shelves, Eddie spotted a half-pint bottle of whiskey tucked away in my back pocket. He walked over to me and softly asked me to step down from the ladder. I did, and he calmly removed the bottle from my pocket, held it up before me and quietly asked, "What's this?"

"It's something I'm taking home to my dad," I said faintly.

"Did you pay for it?"

"No, sir, but I intend to."

"I don't believe you. If you had intended to pay for it, you would have already done so. I think you're stealing it. What else have you taken from me?"

Without waiting for an answer, he said, "Go home and bring back everything you've stolen." Scared and crying, I quickly left the drugstore with no idea of what to do next. I couldn't do as he ordered because there was nothing to bring back, since the Ole Man had drunk the half-pint that I had taken a few days earlier. The candy too was long gone. Nevertheless, I knew I had to bring something back.

As I walked the streets between Eddie and home, I came up with the idea of buying some candy like that I took, going home, waiting awhile and then taking it back to Eddie. So with several bars of candy, I returned to the drugstore. Eddie was busy preparing some prescriptions and didn't bother to look up at me, as I stood before him sweating and scared with the candy in my hand. I was ashamed and feared I was going to lose my job and maybe even be arrested. It seemed an eternity until he finally looked at me, and I handed him the candy. "Are you sure this is everything?" he sternly asked.

I tearfully said, "Yes Sir. And I'm so sorry."

When I told him that the whiskey was meant for the Ole Man, who Eddie knew drank a lot, he paused and softened his manner, causing me to assume that he was shifting the blame from me to the Ole Man. I stood sniffling and said nothing to disabuse Eddie of his apparent suspicion that the Ole Man made me do it. All the same, I felt ashamed of myself because it was solely my idea. After all, "What difference would a couple of bottles of whiskey make? There were so many more of them on the shelves," I thought.

After I promised never to steal from him again, Eddie allowed me to stay on as his clerk. I kept my word, and we had an even better relationship after the theft issue than before. I enjoyed his confidence which he further demonstrated at times when he didn't spend the night at his home and relied upon me to get him to the drugstore on time, with a timely telephone call.

One gloomy afternoon in December, a man walked over to me as I was dusting a display of merchandise. I looked up and asked, "May I help you?" He identified himself as a truant officer and asked my name. My knees buckled; I was terrified. When I told him my name, he asked me why I hadn't attended school and how long had I worked at the drugstore during school hours. Eddie overheard enough to cause him to come out into the store and face the truant officer. The officer told him that I was a truant whom he'd been after for months, explaining that I was only 13 and legally required to attend school and was not permitted to work during school hours. Eddie's voice began to waver, telling the officer that he had no idea I was a truant. He insisted that had he known, he would not have hired me to work during school hours. The truant officer accepted his explanation and decided I was the culprit. Eddie fired me on the spot. As the officer led me from the store, I was full of sorrow and regret, having let Eddie down again. In addition to that, I was scared to death of what the Ole Man was going to do to me when he heard what I had done.

The truant officer took me directly home. As it happened, Babe was there, having returned early from work. Feeling sick with flu symptoms, she listened in disbelief as he laid out his case against me, my bad attendance record and the many written notices he mailed to the Ole Man. In her most assuring manner and voice, Babe declared, "When I tell his daddy what you told me, he'll see to it that he goes to school. Don't you worry about that."

After he left, I pleaded with Babe not to tell the Ole Man. He would be furious to find out that I'd been playing hooky and intercepting his mail. Babe was in a quandary. She felt it her duty to tell him what had happened. But if she did, she knew the Ole Man would tear up my behind. She was not against whippings but fearful of the Ole Man doing it while under the influence. And since he drank everyday, she wondered when she could tell him.

Completely aware of Babe's situation, I quickly promised her that I would return to school, stay there, and work hard to graduate from the 8th. Grade. Having said that, I thought the issue was settled when Babe said nothing more. Then one night while James and the Ole Man were out, Babe, still stunned by the news from the truant officer, brought it up again. "Baby," she said, "what got into yuh? You know yo daddy wants you to stay in school."

"Yeah I know, but Babe I just got tired of going to school," I said.

"And to think you were working full-time," she continued with an expression of shock on her face. "Just wait til I tell Eddie what I think of him for keeping you out of school."

"Don't blame Eddie, please. It wasn't his fault. He didn't know I was fibbing about my age," I said.

She agreed not to confront Eddie but said she had to think about whether or not to tell the Ole Man.

The Ole Man's drinking habit began long before the whiskey theft at Eddie's, starting in his teens. In 1923, when he married Mama, at age 20, he was an alcoholic.

When he was drunk, James and I made fun of him, but that didn't mean I thought little of him. In fact, I thought he was a pretty good guy. When he was sober, he'd sit in our multi-purpose room reading the *St. Louis Post Dispatch* and listening to the radio, trying to keep up with the news about the war in Europe. When he appeared to be in a good mood, I'd ask him to show us a dance he jokingly called "the Mississippi barefoot stump." He was a good dancer and loved doing it.

His first-born son, Ben Jr., was in the Army in Europe. I'd hear the Ole Man say, at times during a pinochle game with Babe and friends, "The way the war is going, it won't be long before Ben Jr. comes home." He talked about my brother as if they were on good terms, but they were far from it. Ben Jr. never accepted the Ole Man's failure to take care of the family. Neither did he cut him any slack for being an alcoholic. They had been close before the family breakup. But after that, he derisively started calling him "the Ole Man", and the name stuck with my two other brothers and me.

Friends of the Ole Man regarded him as very intelligent and knowledgeable. He didn't go beyond the 8th. grade, yet he was self-educated. He was a manners freak, too, teaching my brothers and me to respect our elders by saying "Yes, sir" or "No, sir" and "Yes, mam" or "No, mam." We also learned to address grown-ups as either "Mr.," Mrs.," or "Miss." Occasionally, we thought he carried polite-ness to extremes as when he taught us to call his friend nicknamed "Big Man"—"Mister Big Man."

At 41 the Ole Man was a truck driver for a furniture store, a job that could have helped him get a foothold. But his addiction kept it from happening. On payday despite his best intentions, he and his buddies on the truck would stop at their favorite saloon and drink bourbon until the bartender put the cap on the bottle. He ran a tab at the bar and couldn't make it home with his pay. As Babe put it, "He'd drink it up with a bunch of no good niggers."

It was a rare occasion for him to go into his pocket and pull out some change for James and me to buy soda or ice cream. Not that he didn't want to; he simply didn't have it. But no matter how much he drank, he kept a job and didn't seem to miss much time. James and I looked forward to the times he'd promise us a dime or more for finding bottles of whiskey he'd stashed away in forgotten places in the apartment.

Despite the times I laughed at him stumbling up the street "Drunk as Cooter Brown" trying to make it home, I respected him and felt sorry for him whenever I'd hear him apologizing to Babe for screwing up his money and coming home drunk. I really believed he wanted to do better and even tried to do better. But it never got beyond good intentions. I saw him as a good man who was constantly struggling to do the right thing—but simply couldn't take care of business.

Back in 1938, Mama—who had cried a river of tears since her teenage mar-riage to him—became fed up with the Ole Man's drunken abuse and locked him out one day while he was away. She changed the lock on the door, and when he returned that night and discovered that his key didn't fit the lock, she told him through the closed door, in effect, hit the road Ben and don't come back no more.

After they split up, my two oldest brothers, Ben Jr. and Joseph, stayed with Mama while James and I went to live with the Ole Man. At the time, Mama didn't envision the separation as a permanent arrangement, hoping the Ole Man would stop drinking, become repentant, seek a reconciliation and return to her as a rehabilitated man. But Mama got it all wrong. She didn't know about Babe whom he met at his new lodgings after being locked out. Nor did she know that Babe, a.k.a. Pauline, was twenty-something, a good cook and housekeeper, a lover of children—and enamored of the Ole Man.

On a cold morning in January, 1945, I headed out for Waring School deter-mined to keep my promise to Babe to get back in school and graduate in June. The school had moved to a newly constructed building about four blocks away from home. The route to school was not scenic. The streets were littered with broken glass, pieces of metal, paper, cans, bottles, and other debris strewn about and awaiting collection by the scavengers for the wartime defense industries. But the trip wasn't all bad. The sounds of music coming from storefronts and other places enroute countered the ugliness of the streets. On different days going to school and returning home, I could hear Louis Jordan's "Is You Is Or Is You Ain't My Baby;" Nat King Cole's "Straighten Up And Fly Right;" Ella Fitzgerald's "Into Each Life Some Rain Must Fall," Erskine Hawkins' "Cherry;" and Dinah Washington's "Evil Gal Blues." This compelling music took much of the meanness out of the streets.

My teacher, Miss James, a heavyset good-natured lady, always greeted the class with a cheerful good morning. I was determined to be of good cheer also and abide the ritualism, uniformity and tediousness of school. After starting each day with the "Pledge of Allegiance" Miss James led us in an emotionally rousing rendition of a song that made me feel good and primed for a day of study. She taught us to sing it with such ferver that it resonated throughout the morning and filled me with pride. The song, "Lift Every Voice And Sing" written by James Weldon Johnson and his brother John Rosamond Johnson, was known as the "Negro National Anthem." Here is a sample of its lyrics:

> Lift every voice and sing, till earth and heaven ring,
> Ring with the harmonies of Liberty;
> Let our rejoicing rise, high as the listening skies,
> Let it resound loud as the rolling sea.
> Sing a song full of the faith that the dark past has taught us,
> Sing a song full of the hope that the present has brought us,
> Facing the rising sun, of our new day begun,
> Let us march on till victory is won.
> Stony the road we trod, bitter the chastening rod,
> Felt in the days when hope unborn had died;
> Yet with a steady beat, have not our weary feet
> Come to the place for which our fathers sighed?

3

Betwixt And Between

After returning to school, I got another job as a delivery boy, in a middle-class white neighborhood. The store was owned by two brothers who, like Eddie, were Jewish, and that's where the similarity ended.

The Roger brothers were strictly business, especially the older one who laid out my duties in detail. When there were no deliveries to be made, I had to dust the stock, remove litter from the floor, keep the basement tidy and make myself generally useful—and no killing time chatting with the kids at the soda fountain.

I was glad to be working again and had no problem until the soda jerk quit and the brothers had to replace him. I had often substituted for him—making malted milks, banana splits and other ice cream dishes—when he was either late or absent. I thought it was a great after-school job. And I wanted it badly. So after a couple of days passed without a replacement, I applied for it. Having the final word, the older brother turned me down, claiming "the customers won't accept a Negro soda jerk." Sorely disappointed, I didn't believe for a moment that the customers cared that I was black. And for a long time, I wondered about his real reason for denying me the job.

Late one evening in February, after finishing work and bicycling home, I found Mama and Joseph waiting for me in front of the house. Over the past seven years that I'd been with the Ole Man and Babe, I'd seen very little of Mama. Seeing her there was a huge surprise! Why had she come? I didn't have a clue.

In her inimitable style of communication—laced with authority—she explained that she had come to get me, and I should pack my things and come with her. I was shocked into silence and obedience as we climbed the stairs. I was certain her unannounced appearance—never mind her intentions—would create quite a stir and uproar. As I unlocked the door and they followed me into the apartment, the tension mounted.

Before Mama could say anything, Babe, speaking in her customarily loud and angry voice when vexed, stared at Mama and asked, "What the hell are you doing here?"

The Ole Man, standing next to Babe—and sober—waved his hand before her face and said, "Babe, please calm down."

At this point Mama said, "I've come for George. I want him to live…"

Babe cut her off saying, "What the hell do you mean you come for George?" The Ole Man told Babe to let Mama talk. But Babe was enraged and yelled, "You gave him up and now you say you come for him. You better get out of my house!"

The Ole Man stepped in between Babe and Mama, again telling Babe to let Mama speak. Mama explained, "with weight on her voice" as she liked to say, that she was unable to care for me and James when she sent us to the Ole Man, but now that she was able to take one of us back, she'd come for me. This made no difference to Babe. She remained furious and said I couldn't go with Mama. But the Ole Man intervened taking Mama's side, telling her I could go with her, but he wanted me to stay in nearby Waring School and not to transfer to a school near her. After she agreed, I packed some of my things and left with her and Joseph. It had been a bad scene for Babe, and I felt sorry for her. But when all was said and done, I knew I wasn't leaving Babe for good but would find a way to alternate between her and Mama.

James was not home to witness the battle of the mamas. When I told him what had happened, I sensed he didn't like it that Mama hadn't come for him too. He never liked Mama sending him to live with the Ole Man and showed it. Tension was continual between him and Babe. When she got after him for something, he'd defiantly snap back at her with, "You ain't my mama."

Moving in with Mama didn't cause much of a practical difference in my life. I continued to attend Waring School, and at various times I went there not from Mama's apartment but from Babe's apartment where I often spent the night. After school, I'd return to Babe's, get my bicycle and ride it to the drugstore. When I finished work, occasionally I'd go to Mama's and sometimes I'd go to Babe's. Mama's attention was divided between me, Joseph and Mrs. Nicks, a mother figure to her, who was seriously ill. My freedom never became an issue, and I continued to come and go as I pleased without Mama questioning or challenging me.

Mama was hoping, bit by bit, to reunite the family, first me, then James, and maybe down the road—even the Ole Man. I sensed her strong desire to see us all together once again as a family, even though her life with the Ole Man had been hard and unhappy.

Years after I'd become a man, she told me that she married at 18 while pregnant with Ben Jr. and moved into an already crowded household with Grandma Joanna. Grandma was kind and helpful, but Maggie, one of the Ole Man's sisters, often antagonized and bossed her around. Not knowing she was pregnant, most of Mama's own kinfolk told her not to marry the Ole Man because he wasn't good enough for her. And after she married him anyway, they said that's your "red wagon and you'll have to pull it."

She weathered storm after storm until she finally sought help from her sister, Jesse. Aunt Jesse told her not to take anymore abusive treatment from the Ole Man and Aunt Maggie and to "Move out of that house." Mama got in touch with her sister Florence in St. Louis and asked about job and housing opportunities there. Aunt Florence encouraged Mama to come to St. Louis to start a new life. Pregnant with James in September 1929, Mama left my brothers with grandma and took off for St. Louis. Immediately after her arrival, with the help of her sister, she found a place to stay in a rooming house. And within a few weeks the Ole Man came, bringing Ben Jr. and Joseph with him.

Mama said the first few years in St. Louis were difficult for them, but she believed Jesus was guiding her each step of the way. Mama gave birth to James 2 months after her arrival in St. Louis, and 14 months later, I was born. Fortunately, by then, the Ole Man had a steady job waiting tables at a country club.

In November 1932, Mama and the Ole Man joined Calvary Baptist Church. The Ole Man soon became a deacon. Although they were both religious, Mama's perspective was different from his. Unlike him, she habitually gave scriptural or spiritual meaning to secular ideas and events. If, for instance, a man was accidentally hit by a car while crossing the street, Mama might say it was no accident but that the man was atoning for sinful behavior.

Not long after James was born, Mama worked part-time as a domestic. A few years later, she began to work full-time for a woman, Mrs. Illa, about whom she spoke reverently for many years. Over a 10 year period, she worked 4 to 5 days per week washing and ironing clothes, housecleaning, and cooking dinner. This was a time when white women in University City expected a lot for the meager dollar-per-day paid in wages. Mama had just come from Mississippi and was glad to get the job which she saw as providential. And to Mama, Mrs. Illa was a guardian angel.

Back in 1938, when Mama sent me to live with the Ole Man, I was neither displeased nor saddened. Mama wasn't fun to be around, looking at things the way she did and expecting strict obedience. Besides, I saw a picture of James, who was sent to the Ole Man a few weeks ahead of me, in a new suit. Hopeful of getting new clothes too, I was ready to go.

My relationship with Babe started with the Ole Man saying, "This is Babe" and Babe saying she was happy that I was going to live with them. I knew from the start that I was going to like her. Soon after my arrival, we moved to a larger place where Babe told everybody that James and I were her sons and I was the baby. Right away I was able to appreciate the difference between the personalities and dispositions of Mama and Babe. It didn't take long for me to find out that I could easily cut a deal and get my way with Babe.

At the time Mama came to reclaim me from the Ole Man and Babe, I'd lived with them for seven years and enjoyed freedom to do pretty much what I wanted. Mama's sincerity of purpose touched me. But it was too late because I was not the 14 year old boy she envisioned. He didn't exist. Yet I went along with her out of love and sympathy, knowing I would divide my time between her and Babe—and have my way with both of them.

I liked the West End and was glad Mama lived there. She lived in a low rent apartment on North Taylor Avenue situated in a neighborhood with a wide range of black folk, from the unskilled and uneducated to surgeons and professors. Being accustomed to Mill Creek where colored folk were either low income or no income, I was really impressed.

But the Ville, a distinctive part of the West End, grabbed me even more. It was a self-contained community, the promised land for those black folk striving for a middle-class lifestyle. A good work ethic, a steady and decent paying job, good credit, self-discipline, and a desire to move up was the ticket to the Ville. It was an island paradise in a sea of white supremacy and racial exclusion. There, within 35 or 40 square blocks, colored folk, with huge portraits of Booker T. Washington prominently displayed on the walls of their fine brick homes, prospered as businessmen, professionals, and skilled workers.

While growing up and even afterwards, there was little reason for many of its residents to go outside the Ville for anything because it had its own hospital, physicians, attorneys, schools, a college, churches, a movie theater, drugstores, grocery stores, undertakers, a clothing store, a cleaners, taverns, restaurants, barbershops, ice cream parlors, a furniture store, a tailor, and a gas station. Many black kids grew up in the Ville with no contact at all with white kids or white people in general.

Located over a barbershop, Mama's apartment was cozy and bright, with its two bedrooms, a living room, kitchen and bathroom. I especially liked the bathroom with its hot and cold running water and cheeriness. Her apartment was on a commercial street with small businesses of one kind or another, including taverns, barbershops, candy shops, a seafood restaurant and a poolroom. It was a busy street, bustling at times yet clean and safe.

Though I was only 14 and underage, getting into the poolroom was no problem. After finishing work at the drugstore, sometimes I'd stop there and work on my game. Occasionally racial intermingling took place, despite Jim Crow, when a few white sharpshooters showed up with their entourage and played against their colored counterparts for big bucks. It was really showtime when that happened.

One night shortly after midnight and just before the poolroom emptied, the cops came in and busted the owner and some guys shooting craps in the back room. Just as the cops rushed in, I was grabbed—while ambling out—and about to be thrown into the paddy wagon when one of the cops looked me in the face and snarled, "How old are you?" When I answered, "14," he yelled, "Get the hell out of here, and if I ever catch you in there again, I'll kick your ass!" Scared, I ran home to Mama's place.

My curiosity about different races of people inspired me to visit a nearby office of St. Elizabeth's Catholic Parish on Taylor and Cook. I'd heard that Catholic schools were racially mixed, and I wanted to see inside a school in which everybody was not of the same race. But it turned out that the parish school was not there but downtown nearer to the Ole Man's, and even more disappointing, it too was racially segregated.

When the 1944-45 school year ended, I was enjoying life with my 2 mothers: freedom and independence at Babe's and the niceties of Mama's apartment and neighborhood. Mama got to know me better and saw that I had a mind of my own, and that I was going to continue living, at least part-time, with the Ole Man and Babe.

4

Unbounded

Graduation day, June 12, 1945, finally arrived to put an end to grade school. Wearing my new suit, I happily attended graduation exercises. The program was held in the auditorium of nearby Vashon High School, the school to which I was going in the fall and the one for colored kids living east of Grand Avenue. Babe was happy and proud that I stuck with it and finished. The Ole Man was pleased and accepted it as something he'd taken for granted, and so it wasn't as big a deal with him as it was with Babe. Mama's attitude was pretty much the same as the Ole Man's. The day passed with little celebration within the family, but I didn't feel let down, for I was extremely pleased to have grade school behind me.

Before starting high school in the fall, I wanted to do something especially interesting and fun. But being pretty much a loner, I didn't have any pals to do it with. It would have been nice if James and I had been buddies because we had a lot in common, each eager to learn about what lay beyond the horizon. But our personalities and temperaments conflicted, since I was laid-back and easy going, and he was uptight and domineering. Our relationship was kind of touch and go, and I wasn't always sure of what to expect from him. He treated me as if he was 14 years older rather than 14 months, wanting to lead and expecting me to follow. I could say, "Let's go swimming," and he'd say, "No, let's go to a movie." Or I might say, "Let's go see a movie," and he'd say, "No, let's go swimming." His imperious attitude kept us from being buddies.

A full-time job for the summer was much more promising than hanging out with James. So I decided to look for work. I was 5 feet, 9 inches tall and weighed 126 pounds. Tall enough, I thought, to easily pose as 17 years old and get a regular adult-type job. I soon found one at Burgess Printing Company in downtown St. Louis near the river. My job was kind of fun, using a baling machine to bind waste paper into bales. After a few paydays, I felt so independent and grown up that I opened a savings account at First National Bank and threw away my piggy bank and cigar box.

I had settled into my job when I received a letter from James telling me how things were going for him. I knew he was away, but had no idea he was staying with an aunt in Chicago while working during the summer. He wrote that it was a great place to live and have fun. It sounded so good that I wanted to check it out. So I wrote back and asked him if he thought I could get a summer job there also. In late July he sent me a letter saying he would help me find work and encouraged me to come. I didn't ask, but I wondered why he didn't tell me of his intention to spend the summer in Chicago.

After thinking about it for a couple of days, and being willing to hang out with James on his terms, I told Babe I wanted to go to Chicago. No problem. And if it comes up, she'll tell the Ole Man, she said. When I called James to tell him I was coming, he said he'd meet me at the bus terminal.

Having heard that colored folk were treated better in Chicago than in St. Louis, I was really looking forward to going. James wrote that black people could go to the same movie theaters, restaurants and other public places on an equal basis with white folk. Chicago sounded like a great city, but being from the "Show Me State," I wanted to see it for myself.

Seated voluntarily in the back of the Greyhound bus, I began my journey to Chicago one morning with a spectacular view of the Mississippi River, as we crossed the bridge into East St. Louis, Illinois. This was my second crossing, and I was thrilled, turning my head from right to left trying to trace the river's twisting flow from north to south.

As the bus moved farther north, we passed through a lot of charming little towns. Upon approaching Champaign for a rest stop, the sound of bell music filled the air and continued throughout the stop at the terminal. The music was so beautiful that I stepped off the bus to hear it better and look for its source. While strolling in front of the terminal, I stopped a passing boy and asked him where the music was coming from. He said it was coming from the chimes at the university where they were played daily and could be heard just about all over town. I had never heard of chimes or chime music and listened attentively to what he was saying. A man standing within earshot joined the conversation, adding that the music was coming from the bell tower on the campus of the University of Illinois. Carried away by the music and conversation, I was in no hurry to board the bus. When the bus pulled away from the terminal, the chimes were playing "Beautiful Dreamer," not as soulfully as Ray Charles may have done it, but surely as sweetly and melodiously as Stephen Foster intended.

Shortly after leaving Champaign, the bus pulled into the Chicago terminal about mid-afternoon. James was there to meet me just as he said he would. After a brief greeting, he said that he wanted to take me to a private employment agency nearby. He was certain they could find me a job right away. So off we went. And he was right. The agency woman said she had an immediate opening for a kitchen helper at a country club. And with my approval, she made arrangements for me to go directly there from the agency. I had only been in Chicago for little more than an hour and already had a job. Wow! I was really impressed—as much with James as with the agency.

Without seeing anything of Chicago beyond the bus terminal, I was on another bus enroute to the country club in La Grange, Illinois, a place southwest of Chicago and about an hour away. It was a very small town and virtually all-white. My interview at the club went well, and I got the job working in the kitchen scrubbing pots and doing other things to help with food preparation. This was a great job with room, board and salary! Thanks to my "big" brother James.

With the help of the friendly cooks and others, it took less than a week to learn my way around the kitchen. Everybody made me feel welcome and at ease. All I had to contend with was the endless flow of pots and pans.

On my first morning at the club, I awoke early and went out to enjoy the smell and sight of the great expanse of freshly cut grass. What a place! For the next several days, either before or after work, I'd roam the humongous grounds of the club. It was so picturesque. It blew my mind to see for the first time all that wide open space with fairways, greens, and rolling hills. While roving, I discovered a few ponds and noticed some white kids gathered about them.

One day when I wandered over to one of the ponds to have a good look at it, one of the kids there called out a friendly hello. I walked over to him, and as we began to chat, a few other kids gathered about us. Smiling and in a laid-back manner, they asked me who I was, where I came from and what I was doing there. They really appeared interested in me and what I had to say. These kids made me feel welcome and encouraged me to join their little group.

I quickly learned that they were into much more than just hanging out at the pond. Some of them were caddying and learning how to play golf, having been taught the fundamentals by the club's golf pro. Jonathan, one of my buddies who wanted to be like Byron Nelson, taught me how to stand, to swing a club, and to putt. But despite his earnest teaching and motivational efforts, I lacked the interest to give it my best shot. A missed opportunity. Too bad.

I had a better time hanging out at the pond and trying to retrieve stray golf balls. It was not only fun finding the balls under water, but the golf pro paid us for each ball that wasn't too banged up. Kids who swam the best dove for the balls in the deepest parts of the pond, while other kids waded close to the shore to fetch the balls. Not knowing how to swim, I tried to stay near the shore, standing with my shoulders above the water.

One day, while reaching down into the pond for a ball as I held onto a log, it began to revolve and float slowly into the deeper parts of the pond. The more I tried to stop that log from floating, the more it revolved and floated. Scared, I knew that I was in deep trouble, yet wanting to be cool, I didn't show it by calling for help. Instead I just kept hugging that log which had by then made its way into deep water. Jonathan yelled, "Are you okay?" I was too busy trying to keep up with the turning log to answer. Suddenly he and a couple of kids swam out and steered the log and me back to shore. Without saying a word, they then swam off in different directions. Still insisting on being cool, I never told them how frightening it was.

James and I had been in touch by telephone, and after I'd been at the club for about three weeks, we got together in Chicago. He met me at the bus terminal, and from there we strolled in the Loop. There, I'd stop every step or so just to stare at the huge department stores, cafeterias, movie theaters and other places that caught my attention and seemed so inviting. I had seen similar places in St. Louis, although perhaps on a lower scale, but, because of Jim Crow, they had little meaning to me.

Entranced, I stood in front of a cafeteria with gigantic windows and enormous neon signs. "Lets go in," I said to James. The spaciousness, cleanliness and orderliness of the place was breathtaking and gave me pause, causing James to nudge me forward in the direction of the counter and food display. The very idea that all a person had to do in this magnificent place was to get a tray, go before the counter and choose whatever he wanted was fantastic.

After more than an hour in the cafeteria, we left and headed for the Chicago Theater. James said it was similar to the Fox Theater in St. Louis, featuring a stage show and a recently released movie. I knew that about the Fox, but I didn't know what it was like to be inside a theater like it. I could only imagine. In fact, there were mornings when I would stop, while walking pass the Fox before it opened, and peer with wonder through its immense glass doors. I could see its spacious refreshment area and its carpeted lobby and staircases. But I didn't know how it felt to be a patron free to move about within its cavernous walls and seated in its deep-cushioned seats. At the Chicago Theater, I no longer had to rely on my imagination to know what it was like to be in a majestic movie theater. James and I purchased tickets, went in, bought popcorn and sat wherever we wanted.

Dick Haymes (a singer James liked) appeared on stage. James was right about Chicago. It was a great city!

Labor Day marked the end of my job at the country club. The fall semester at Vashon High School was about to begin. It was time to return home, but I was in no hurry and took a round-about way back, stopping to visit Mama's sister, Aunt Creasie, in South Bend. This was a good opportunity to meet her and her children, as well as to see this northern Indiana city. At the time, it had a large first generation immigrant population which included Germans, Belgians and Poles, in addition to a growing migrant population of colored people from the South. The bus ride there was no more than a couple of hours from Chicago.

Aunt Creasie, who lived in a small frame house in a low-income neighborhood which was not entirely all-black, welcomed me warmly, saying how pleased she was to see me.

While chatting with me about South Bend, my cousin, Abby, said there were some public places that didn't welcome colored people but that segregation there was not as widespread as in other places in the country. Her complaint was mostly about it being a small town where everybody knew your business.

Niles, Michigan and the beaches along Lake Michigan were only minutes away. While in South Bend, I went to a beach for the first time in my life. It was great fun hanging out with Abby and her friends. I said to one of them, Alice, that I had to return home for high school. She facetiously asked, "Why don't you stay and go to school in South Bend?" Though I took the question as a joke, I did wonder if high schools in South Bend were segregated and asked if they were. She said none of their high schools was all-black or all-white, but that each one had at least a trickle of black or white students.

Intrigued by what Alice said about high schools in South Bend, I seriously wondered if there was a way for me to attend high school there. I could easily get Babe's support, and she would bring the Ole Man around, and Mama would tacitly go along. When I tried the idea on Aunt Creasie, her attitude was why not. So I decided to stick around for a while. I called Babe and talked to her about what I wanted to do and got her okay. Then, instead of returning to St. Louis, I waited until the high schools in South Bend opened for registration, and in the meantime, I got a part-time job as an afternoon porter at the YMCA.

John Adams High School was my school of choice because it looked grand and new. When I showed up to register for classes, I was so daunted by the school's imposing building, its impressive tower, and its environment that I had second thoughts about going ahead. This sprawling school with its lush green campus was stunning and seemed too grandiose to be a high school. I timorously entered the building and made my way to the main office where I was greeted by a pleasant lady who listened carefully as I explained what I wanted to do. She said that I could attend as a nonresident transfer student and my parents would have to pay fees. She didn't know it, but that was the worst thing she could have said because any cost—no matter how small—was formidable. My hope of attending a nonsegregated high school was shattered. That evening I called Babe to tell her I was coming home.

With contrasting images of John Adams High School and Vashon causing me to shudder, the day after returning home, I dragged myself to Vashon and registered for freshmen classes. Without caring, I mindlessly went through the registration process. But it didn't matter because I never attended a single class. Instead, I hid out at home moping, without considering the consequences of skipping school.

The days passed into weeks as I reverted to my former hooky playing behavior, listening to the radio and intercepting the Ole Man's mail from the attendance office. My body was back in the slums of Mill Creek, but my thoughts were elsewhere—on the people I met and the fun I had. Only James knew I dropped out, and he kept it to himself.

Only a couple of months had passed since the Japanese surrendered, and the radio was full of martial music and happy talk about returning servicemen. One day in late October, while listening to music like "Anchors Aweigh," "Halls of Montezuma," and "Stars and Stripes," blaring from the radio, I was stirred by patriotic feelings. Thinking a lot about Ben Jr., I said to James—who was playing hooky and stretched out on the sofa—"I think Ben should be coming home soon." He agreed saying that under the point system because he was married, he should be getting out in a little while. That our oldest brother had fought in the war was a big deal to us. He was our hero, and we looked forward to him coming home.

I was chatty and carried on about the various branches of the military: the Army, Navy, and Marines. "Which do you like best?" I asked James.

"I like the Army," he said as he wrapped a leg over the back of the sofa.

"Ah, how could you like the Army? That uniform is ugly," I said. As the booming sound of "Anchors Aweigh" burst forth from the radio, I started marching across the room shouting, "I like the Navy. What do you think of the Navy's uniform, and don't you just love this music?."

"Not really. And it's too loud," he said, as he stood up to turn it down.

"I think it would be great being in the Navy. If I was old enough, I would join," I said.

As I rattled on, I remembered a huge navy recruitment poster in front of the YMCA in South Bend that read: "Join the Navy and See the World!"

With each passing day, I became more obsessed with the idea, thinking about it daily and wondering if there was a way to join. In order to do so, I'd have to prove I was at least 17. And even then, I'd have to have my parents' consent. I wanted to let James in on my thoughts and get his thinking because he often had good ideas. But for fear he would belittle my ideas and strong feelings about the Navy, I decided to keep my thoughts to myself.

One day it popped into my head that even though the war had ended, guys still had to register for the draft when they reached 18. And I also knew there were lots of guys who were not eager to register. So I figured if I showed up at the draft board claiming to be 18, they'd take my word for it and issue me a draft card which, I believed, was automatic proof of being at least 18. The card would then be my ticket to the Navy, without parental consent. It was a sure thing, but I didn't have the nerve to go to the draft board office. I must have thought about it day and night for a week or more while listening to martial music and marching between the kitchen and living room, imagining myself all dressed up in Navy blues. Then one day I got my courage up and decided to go to the draft board office.

On November 9, 1945, nervous and jittery, at age 14, I went to the draft board office to register for military service. I walked in dressed in my graduation suit and tie and the Ole Man's overcoat. Underneath that heavy woolen coat which broadened my shoulders by inches, I must have looked twenty pounds heavier. Feeling certain I looked 18, I calmly sauntered up to the man at the counter and said I was 18 and had come to register. Without giving me more than a glance, he handed me some forms to fill out. So far so good, I thought. I filled out the forms and returned them. The man looked at them, and to my amazement, he handed me a draft card right on the spot in little more than a few minutes. Amazed, I walked away from the counter. It took awhile to realize my scheme had worked. On the streetcar home, I pulled the card from my wallet and proudly looked at it, more than once.

Since I had to share my joy and happiness with somebody, I let James in on it, by showing him my card. He took it in his hand, looked at it closely and asked, "What's this?," as if he couldn't see.

"It's a draft card," I said.

"Yeah, so what?" he asked.

Though he tried to fake indifference, I knew he wanted to know the story behind the card. So with relish, I told him everything. Knowing I was now eligible for induction into the Army, he asked me if it was my intention to be drafted. I said it was my intention to use the card to join the Navy. His quizzical expression told me he was curious about how I'd do that. But he didn't ask and I didn't say.

It really felt great to have gone to the draft board office and come away with a card. But I wasn't cocky about taking the next step to the Navy Recruiting Station. My height was right for an 18-year-old, but I thought my baby face might cause the recruiter to question my age regardless of the draft card. This trickier part of my scheme caused me to think hard about it and the reason for it. And the more I thought, the more apparent it became that I had to make the next move, for to do otherwise meant remaining in the painfully dull world of St. Louis.

So, with determination to see the real world in my mind, my draft card in my pocket, and the Ole Man's overcoat on my back, I took a streetcar to the Navy Recruiting Station on Locust Street in downtown St. Louis. Upon arriving in front of the station, I stood outside, looking in the window at the various posters, working up the guts to go in. I was spotted by a recruiter who beckoned me inside. Once there, I told him that I had just registered for the draft and was thinking about joining the Navy. The recruiter smiled and cordially said, "Let's see what we can do."

He invited me to sit down and after talking about the advantages of service in the Navy, he gave me some enlistment forms to take home, complete, and return to him. At this point I thought I had it made, but then he gave me a staggering jolt by saying my parents' consent would be needed. This requirement was totally unexpected and confusing—after all, my draft card was supposed to indicate that I was beyond the need of parental consent—but I wasn't about to question the recruiter. With the packet of papers stuffed in my overcoat pocket, I left the recruiting office with a heavy heart. My scheme was doomed, for there was no way Mama and the Ole Man were going to sign me into the Navy.

5

Reviving Hope

Still in shock after I returned home, I plopped down on the sofa and opened the packet of papers. Inattentively looking them over, I felt like tearing them up and throwing them into the trash. I was really confused at this point. Had my scheme hit a dead-end or an awful snag? Luckily nobody was home to notice and question me about my depressed mood. I stuffed the papers back in the envelope, put the packet aside and stretched out on the sofa. Suddenly, like a thunderbolt, Babe came to mind. I wondered if she could sign the papers as my mother. Sure she could, if I could talk her into doing it. And it would work. The idea was so exciting that I jumped up from the sofa, got myself a glass of water and sat thinking about the best way to try and get her to sign the papers.

One night while the Ole Man and James were away, I got a chance to talk to Babe privately. I brought up my failure to go to school in South Bend and why it had been so important to me to go to school there. With a forlorn look on my face, I said I didn't want to go to Vashon. She understood my feelings and was sorry I felt so bad, she said. "But Baby," she added, "you got to go to school." Now that I had her ear and her sympathy, I knew I had to get to the point of her signing me into the Navy.

"Babe I know this may sound crazy, but I want to join the Navy," I said.

"You wanna do what?" she blurted out, as she stopped preparing dinner and sat down next to me at the kitchen table and stared me in the face.

Pleadingly, I said, "They have schools in the Navy to teach and train you to do a lot of stuff. And after only two years, I can come out and keep on going to school under the GI Bill."

"Wait a minute, Baby. They won't take you in the Navy. You ain't old enough," she said warily.

"I could put my age up. That's no problem," I said, without mentioning the draft card.

With a look of I can't believe we're having this conversation, she said, "Let's talk about it later, Baby, I got to get dinner ready."

Even though she said nothing to encourage me, I still felt there was a chance. So I hurriedly filled out the forms and took them back to the recruiter. He gave me more papers and told me to bring them back along with my parents. I told him I was unsure whether the Ole Man could come because he had a drinking problem. "My mother will come," I said. "Try and get him to come, but if he can't, have him sign the papers," he said. Boy, I was glad he said that! Being good at forging the Ole Man's signature meant I had it made. The only thing left to do was to talk Babe into signing as my mother.

Before leaving the recruiting office, the recruiter asked me which branch of the Navy did I want to enlist in, the Steward Branch or the Seaman Branch. I told him it didn't matter as long as I could go to sea. Then he said, "How about the Steward Branch?" Guessing this was the branch that would take me overseas, I answered, "Okay."

After talking to Babe about wanting to join the Navy, I let a couple of days pass before I brought the subject up again. I knew she needed time to think about what I said and felt she would help me if she thought she reasonably could. When I got a chance to talk to her again privately, I brought her up-to-date on what I had done and told her it was all set for me to enlist. "All I need is for you to come with me and sign the papers," I said. She gave me a blank stare and started to say something, but I continued talking. I told her that the recruiter said the Ole Man didn't have to come. She gave me a look of disbelief but hung in there with me, letting me have my say. "Don't worry about a thing," I said, "all you have to do is come with me to the office and sign as my mother, and only you, the recruiter and I would ever know about the signing."

"But what about Madeline...?" she asked, referring to Mama.

Cutting off her line of thought, I replied, "When she finds out I'm in the Navy and sees me doing okay she won't mind."

Time to sign the papers was running out, and I was becoming more uneasy. So I put more pressure on Babe. One morning on her day off, I begged her to come with me to the recruiting office, but she said, "Baby, I don't know." I kept repeating that it meant a lot to me to join the Navy and pleading with her to come with me and sign the papers until she finally gave in.

As soon as we arrived at the office, we were met by the recruiter. Handing him the papers, I introduced Babe as my mother. Babe looked on in complete silence as the recruiter showed her some pamphlets about opportunities in the Navy and repeated what I'd said about the benefits of the GI Bill to veterans. After telling

Babe about the wonderful life I'd have in the Navy, he laid out papers for her signature and mine. Robot-like, Babe signed them, as I looked endearingly at her with a glorious feeling of satisfaction. When the signing was over, we were told that the swearing-in ceremony would take place after all the papers were processed. And I could expect to receive word in the mail about the date and time of the ceremony. He shook hands with us and we left. On the streetcar home, holding Babe's hand, I expressed my gratitude for her help and understanding.

Waiting for word about when to return for the swearing-in ceremony was hard to bear. I needed to talk to somebody about what I was feeling and wanted to share my feelings with Babe, but I didn't because she was still trying to be comfortable with what she had done. So I sweated it out keeping my feelings to myself and waited.

Finally, on a day in the middle of November, I received a letter from the recruitment office. I took the letter from the mailbox and raced up the stairs tightly holding onto it until I entered the apartment and sat down. Excited and nervous, I had trouble opening the envelope. With my dreams riding on the contents of the letter, I tore into the envelope, hoping and praying for good news. I pulled out the letter, and there it was: a date and time for my swearing-in ceremony. No complications. I had been accepted for a two-year enlistment in the Navy. It had worked and I was ecstatic!

When I shared the news with Babe, I could tell she was still having second thoughts about the role she played. I sensed that she didn't want to come to the swearing-in ceremony and didn't ask her. My joy was tempered slightly by the awareness that I had put her on the spot and caused her to do something she dreaded doing.

On my way to the recruiting station for the swearing-in ceremony, I thought about that poster I saw in front of the YMCA in South Bend and how it was the seed that led to this outcome. It was the happiest day of my life. The solemn swearing-in ceremony made me feel patriotic, proud and grown up. It was just great. Following the ceremony, I was given my travel orders; my travel day was put off until Monday, giving me the weekend at home.

That night, I happily shared the day's events with Babe. "Baby," she said with a faint smile, "I sure hope we did the right thing."

I hugged her and said, "We did and I love you. Thanks for helping me. Don't worry, everything is going to be alright. I'll be back as soon as I get a leave. When I return and the Ole Man and Mama see me in my uniform, they'll know I'm okay. Just let daddy think I'm at Mama's. Mama thinks I'm here with you. So she won't miss me."

Looking down at the floor, she said, "Okay Baby."

When James, who had no knowledge of my actual enlistment in the Navy, came home, I handed him the envelope containing my orders.

Grinning, I said, "Look at this."

Shifting glances from the bulky envelope to me, he slowly pulled the papers from within, scanned the top sheet, and calmly asked, "What's this?"

"My orders," I said beaming with pride, "you are now looking at a sailor in the United States Navy."

He didn't asked how it happened, but I knew he wanted the details. Still I didn't tell him because I promised Babe I wouldn't tell anybody. I merely repeated to him what I said to Babe about how I'd tell the Ole Man and Mama later.

6

Trying To Make It Real

On November 20, 1945, with three other recruits—one black and two white—I took a train from Union Station for the Naval Training Center in Bainbridge, Maryland, full of excitement and joy and without the slightest fear. The black recruit, Dennis, an ex-soldier and leader of our little group, carried all the tickets and dining car vouchers—for sleeping in the Pullman section and eating in the dining car. This was my first train ride, and it was first-class all the way. My great adventure into the greater world of possibilities had started off with a big bang.

"Are you guys ready for boot camp?" Dennis asked. "It's gonna be tough on you in the beginning, but you can get through it with flying colors if you do what you're told." He talked about having to get up and go to bed early and other things we'd have to get used to. I wasn't sure of what he was trying to do—scare us or encourage us. But I was committed to doing whatever it took to make it.

The training center was about 40 miles east of Baltimore near the mouth of the Susquehanna River at Chesapeake Bay. It was an immense place that seemed to be completely surrounded by forest. Upon our arrival, Dennis and I were separated from the two other guys. Dennis said they were barracked with other apprentice seamen, and that we would be assigned to a barracks with black guys in training to become steward mates. Although the ex-soldier had hinted at it on the train, I was still surprised to learn that the Steward Branch was made up entirely of nonwhite sailors and that black and white sailors were segregated at the training center.

The recruiter didn't tell me colored and white sailors were separated in the Navy. Maybe he didn't think it was important to mention it, inasmuch as colored and white folk were separated in St. Louis. Nor did he explain what it meant to be a steward mate. He merely said that if I wanted to go to sea, I should sign up for the Steward Branch.

After a few weeks in boot camp I heard some guys in the barracks talking about both branches of the Navy. They said that because of segregation, colored sailors in the Seaman Branch didn't serve on seagoing warships. Only colored sailors in the Steward Branch did since their duty was to take care of shipboard officers' quarters and mess; that is to say, to make the officers' bed, keep his quarters clean and to cook and serve his food.

Guys talked in a matter-of-fact manner about their work, without showing it made a difference to them. But one steward mate pointed out that colored newspapers had criticized the use of colored sailors solely for this purpose aboard warships and mockingly referred to them as "seagoing bellhops." All of that talk held my attention, and it took a while to get over how I unknowingly joined a segregated Navy in fleeing a segregated city. Yet I thought it was a good trade-off. I was ready to be a sea-going bellhop on a segregated ship if that was what it took to see the world.

After the first day of our arrival at the barracks, I don't remember seeing Dennis anymore. I guessed he was put in a more advanced company because of his prior military service. My company was made up of raw recruits who were facing ten weeks of boot camp training. It didn't take long to learn that a "boot," as each recruit was called, was regarded as the lowliest member of the Navy. It was said that in neither the Steward nor the Seaman Branch did a boot deserve to be called "sailor."

We brand-new recruits were organized into an all-black company and told that we would act as a team throughout boot camp. We'd train together, eat together, live in the same barracks and gripe together from that moment on. That was cool because I felt I could hold my own, believing the differences in our ages were no big deal. However, what I failed to see at the time was that those guys had some experiences with girls and women that I had yet to even imagine. For the next ten weeks, I heard about them. And whether they were real or made up, they made an impression.

After assignment to barracks and company, we were taken to a place to get clothes. There, we moved in a line before a long counter, as if we were in a cafeteria, and for starters we received shoes, socks, underwear, dungarees, caps, a ditty bag, and a seabag. Afterwards, we returned to our barracks, showered, put on our new clothes and went to the mess hall for lunch. After lunch a petty officer gave us an overview of the boot camp program—its objectives and our responsibilities. We were also given basic information about reveille, taps, muster, and eating at the mess hall.

Life in the barracks was awkward at first because it lacked privacy. A bunch of guys using the head—bathroom—together and guys in the shower boasting about and playing with their private parts took time to become accustomed to.

Often in the late afternoon after returning from dinner and while stretched out on my bunk thinking about some of the stuff that had happened during the day, I'd listen to guys gabbing about one thing or another. These guys, like many others in the company, were from the South and were funny in the way they talked. A handful of them were high school graduates. Some said they enlisted in order to avoid induction in the Army, while others said the Navy offered them a good life. All of them wanted to go to sea and, unlike me, knew the difference between the two branches of the Navy—before enlisting.

As I listened to them, I found myself thinking that even though these guys were from three to six years older than I, they didn't seem any smarter. But each time I began to feel smug, they'd move on to some topic that brought home to me how much I didn't know—and had to learn. If they knew the depth of my ignorance about women, sex, drinking, smoking and cussing, they would have shunned me like a disease. For fear that I might reveal my innocence, I kept my mouth shut and listened. None of them ever found out how much I'd learned from them.

Despite more than an hour hopping around like a rabbit, naked or near naked with our clothes bundled up under our arms as we moved forward on line waiting to be called, the medical exam was no problem. The dental exam, on the other hand, was something else and caused me to sweat.

I'd heard that wisdom teeth grew according to one's age, and by 17 or 18 a person was supposed to have a definite number of these teeth. If he had less than this number he was younger than 17 or 18. So during the dental examination, because I was only 14 I was certain the dentist would notice that I didn't have the number of teeth a 17 or 18 year-old guy was supposed to have—and therefore know that I was underage for the Navy. So when the dentist began his examination, I sat in fear of detection. But, to my astonishment he examined my teeth and passed me on without comment or questions. Nevertheless, I believed my underage status had been found out and sooner or later I'd hear about it. Afterwards for days—that seemed like weeks—I waited in fear thinking any day now, I'll get the word to come and see somebody about being kicked out of the Navy. But the bad news never came. Boy, I was so relieved and happy.

Life in boot camp wasn't bad. It didn't take long to get used to living with a bunch of guys in a barracks, getting up before dawn and eating navy chow. However, there was one thing I had trouble with—fire drills in the middle of the night. One morning about three o'clock, the fire alarm sounded and fire marshalls hurriedly and noisily entered the barracks seeing to it that everyone had quickly gotten up and assembled outside. Ignoring all the commotion, I stayed in my bunk determined to sleep throughout the entire event. Suddenly my bunk rocked and rolled like a ship on a stormy sea. The company commander responsible for all the turbulence angrily shouted, "Get your ass out of here, now!" As I scrambled to obey, I looked about the deserted barracks and realized I was the only boot there. I was scared and felt stupid as I ran out of the barracks in full view of my company.

Long after the fire drill was over and my company had returned to the barracks, I was still outside undergoing punishment. On a predawn winter day in a wooded place overlooking the Susquehanna, I, a lonely sniveling boot, jogged in front of the barracks until the company commander came—an hour later—and ordered me to stop. Though my dislike for fire drills in the middle of the night never abated, my rebellion against them ended on that cold, lonely winter morning.

Although our ten-week training program differed from that of seamen, some areas of instruction were similar. We were, for example, trained in close order drill and taught something about gas masks, rifles, rowing and swimming. Also like seamen, we were given instruction in personal health care with emphasis on the use of condoms. It was during one of these instructional sessions that I learned a "short arm inspection" had nothing to do with a hand-held weapon.

Close order drill was my favorite training activity. It took place before and after lunch almost daily. It was great fun marching to the call and response pattern of the drill instructor while staying in step. He would call and the company would respond

"You Had A Good Home But You Left."

"Your Right"

"You want to go back but you can't"

"Your Right"

"But Now You're Living The Navy Way And Will Til The End Of Your Life. So Sound Off"

"Sound Off"

"Sound Off"

"Sound Off, One, Two, Three Four"

I thought this one which referred to a town a few miles down the road was the coolest of them all:

"I've Got A Gal In Perryville"

"She won't [silence]But Her Sister Will"

"She Won't [trampling feet] But Her Sister Will"

"Sound Off"

"Sound Off"

"Sound Off"

"Sound Off, One, Two Three Four"

Often during close order drill, I was reminded of those times at home, only a couple of months ago, when I was listening to "Anchors Aweigh" and marching around the living room with an imaginary rifle on my shoulder. It was as though I pushed a button which caused imagination and reality to merge.

Rowing on the Susquehanna River, like predawn fire drills, was not one of my favorite things. I would have felt different about it if it had been midsummer instead of midwinter. My buddy, Earl, a big, tall guy from Chicago, didn't care for it either. On his soapbox one morning as we assembled prior to muster, he said to a few of us, "This morning we're gonna learn a skill we ain't never gonna use. Now ain't that a bitch!"

"But," one of the other guys said, "suppose you were on a ship that was in trouble and the crew had to leave it. Wouldn't you be glad you knew how to row a boat?"

Earl sneeringly replied, "That ain't about to happen. And even if it did, rowing boats is the white boys' job. You ain't no white boy; that ain't your job!"

Most of the guys disagreed with Earl's premise, but everybody agreed when he complained about how cold it felt on the river and exclaimed, "Man, it's colder than a well digger's ass in the Klondike!"

We sat in the long boat—two men abreast on a plank bench and an oar in each man's hand. There were eight men or so positioned in this way. The idea was to propel the boat forward via coordinated movement of the oars as prescribed by the coxswain seated in the bow. Unable or unwilling to concentrate sufficiently on the learning task, our crew had much difficulty raising its performance level. But it didn't seem to matter to the coxwain. He was undeterred and determined to stay on course with his prepared set of instructions, taking us through the motions until we completed the required number of hours on the river.

In the poolroom of the recreation hall, I was right at home. The problem was there were too few tables for all the guys who wanted to play, and you had to sign up for the next available table. One time a boot tried to bully me out of my right to the next table by stepping up to the table with his cue and gathering the balls. Ignoring him, I picked up a cue, held it by its thinner end, and moved toward the table with the rack in my hand. He gave me a mean look and growled, "Give me that rack. You little skinny son-a-fa-bitch." Other boots including Earl looked on to see what was going to happen. With my ears ringing from the name calling, I calmly stood at a pocket of the table, holding the rack in one hand and the cue stick in the other, warily watching the bully across the table. Despite his outright size advantage, I was determined to hit him as hard as I could with the stick if he made a move to hurt me. Suddenly, he strutted away from the table muttering, "Ah, fuck you."

Because of my spindly body and baby face, a few boots challenged me, thinking I was a pushover. But I slowly built a reputation for being a guy who would not back down. I believed that standing up to a would-be tough guy would make him think twice before messing with me.

Generally, life in boot camp was not bad, although it could be physically demanding and boring at times. Barracks life was routine and orderly. Taps meant lights out at 10:00 P.M. and reveille meant getting up at 5:30 A.M. On a few occasions, the company commander would storm into the barracks a minute or so after taps, yelling, "Lights out! And I don't want to hear a mouse piss on cotton."

Sometimes there was no training schedule posted in advance, so we didn't always know what was in store until the day it was to happen. One day I was happily surprised to learn that our company was meeting with the swimming instructors who were setting up an instructional program for nonqualified swimmers. We came together in a place with a swimming pool the width and length of a football field and seemingly as deep as an ocean. Boots who claimed they could swim were offered the opportunity to demonstrate their ability. Earl said he could swim, got his chance to prove it, and was excused from taking swimming instruction. He made fun of me for not knowing how to swim. "Yeah, laugh now, but I'll have the last laugh when I learn to swim better than you," I said. All boots who couldn't swim had to take swimming lessons and were designated nonqualified swimmers (NQS). Although I liked the idea of learning to swim, I didn't like it that the instructional sessions were scheduled at night in mid-January.

After four weeks of training and with little advance notice, our company was given a holiday leave of seven days. Looking forward to going home for Christmas and Babe seeing me in uniform, I packed my seabag, put on my dress blues and took the train for St. Louis. As I sat looking out of the window, my head was full of thoughts about some of the things that had happened. And I freaked out at the awareness that graduation from grade school, experiences in Chicago, La Grange, South Bend, and Bainbridge had all taken place within 6 months.

When my train pulled into Union Station at St. Louis, the large number of servicemen coming and going caught my eye. Most of them were veterans wearing their ribbons and medals, and they looked as though they'd just returned from overseas. There were also some sailors with a yellow patch of Ruptured Duck sewn over their right breast pocket—which meant they had completed their service and were discharged from the Navy. Civilians in the station were especially courteous and respectful to all the guys in uniform, including me. For me, a 14 year-old boy, this was heady stuff. I felt great being there among those guys. Perfect strangers were smiling and deferential in many little ways. In fact, there was such an aura of togetherness in the station that I stopped in Fred Harvey's Restaurant for lunch without fear of being discriminated against—and was served!

After leaving Fred Harvey's I got in one of the colored-folk taxis loading up outside the station and headed for Babe and the Ole Man. Babe was expecting me and was home waiting when I arrived. As she stood in the doorway gazing at me in my uniform, she broke into tears. After a few seconds of silence, she said, "Baby you look so grown! But you still ain't nothing but my baby." We hugged and kissed. James showed up minutes later, checked me out, and was clearly struck by the sight of me in my Navy dress blues, saying, "Not bad, not bad."

He filled me in on what had happened during the four weeks I'd been away, telling me that Mama was still mourning the death of her friend Mrs. Nicks. This was not a good time to show up at her door in my uniform, and so I passed up a visit with her and Joseph, who also didn't know I was in the Navy.

Babe said she hadn't told the Ole Man I was in the Navy, leaving it to me. And there was no hurry for me to tell him, for—as it happened—when briefly running into him in the apartment, I was never in uniform.

At a drugstore buying a pack of cigarettes, one afternoon, I chatted with the clerk, Joan, who seemed stuck on me in my uniform. Being friendly, upbeat and lively, Joan—a chubby, light brown-skinned teenager—was a real charmer. It was easy for me to talk to her because she did most of the talking, saying she liked my pea-coat and that she was going to college.

Joan had finished Sumner High School and was going to Howard University in the fall.

Meanwhile, she was working to save money. She was so together, knowing what she wanted to do with herself and planning and working toward that end. I was fascinated and wanted to know more about her. Before leaving the drugstore, I knew her telephone number and that she lived with her mother.

Beyond merely chatting with them, I didn't yet know how to make out with girls. Nor did I know if the how to get into a girl's pants manual put out by the guys in boot camp applied to a strait laced girl like Joan. I was sorrowfully lacking in ability to size her up as a willing sex partner. She was friendly, but what did that mean. Would she or wouldn't she? I couldn't figure it out. And I couldn't ask her directly, for that wasn't the respectful thing to do. I believed that unless a girl gave a guy an invitation to go for it, he should be cool. But how could I, at my level of innocence, know when Joan was being invitational?

Having decided to explore the question, I called her and we went out a couple of times. She continued to do most of the talking and invariably chose the subjects. I listened with indifference and wondered if she would ever get around to the subject of sex. I brought her to the Ole Man's apartment once when nobody was there. As we sat on the sofa chatting, I moved closer to her and put my arm around her shoulders. She showed no displeasure and continued talking about her hopes and dreams. As she talked, I snuggled close, putting my cheek on hers. Cautiously, I placed my lips on hers, and when she didn't resist, I drew her closer in a warm embrace and kissed her. She responded nicely, leading me to think an invitation was imminent, but she freed herself from my embrace and commenced to chatter. Throwing caution to the wind, I quickly drew her close again, kissed her, and put my hand on her exposed knee and slowly began to move my hand underneath her skirt and upward on her thigh. Before I could reach the target, she suddenly put her hand on mine, stopped the advance, the kiss, and the embrace—and began to prattle again. Totally confused and discouraged, I gave up the idea of sex with Joan and remained a virgin sailor for the duration of my visit home.

The novelty of being home in my uniform wore off in 5 or 6 days, and I was eager to return to boot camp.

After returning, I looked forward to the start of my swimming classes. Ever since almost drowning at that country club in La Grange, I wanted to learn how to swim. Now there was a powerful incentive to learn, for each boot had to qualify as a swimmer in order to graduate from boot camp. Anyone failing to do so would remain in boot camp until passing the qualifying test. The scuttlebut was that portions of the test were scary—like the part where a guy had to jump off a narrow platform about fifty feet above the water. I tried to bury the thought of that part of the test and to think merely about learning how to swim—over the next four or five weeks.

In January, 1946, our company began receiving instruction at Steward School. The school's mission was to train us in the skill and art of attending to the food and lodging needs of officers at sea. This school was not in the league with Cordon Blue or Cornell's Hotel School, but it was at least a formalized attempt to provide steward mates with some training. Prior to 1943, steward mates received hardly any training at all.

7

High Noon In New York

On a very cold morning in February, about a week before the end of boot train-ing, our company took the qualifying swimmer's test. There were dozens of guys in the long circuitous line leading to the base of the fifty-foot tower above a gigantic swimming pool. At times the atmosphere was spine-tingling, with some guys visibly trembling with fear at the mere sight of the tower. I tried to avoid looking at them, for I was scared enough. One after another the line spewed out a boot to climb the dreaded tower. Qualified swimmers were at the head of the line followed by people like me—nonqualifying swimmers who had taken swimming lessons.

I watched nervously as each guy—fully dressed—climbed the ladder to the top. Each boot stood on the narrow platform, with a proctor standing alongside him, and suddenly jumped, splashed into the water and disappeared. I paid atten-tion as he emerged and attempted to reach the side of the pool by swimming around a line of rafts, small boats, tubes and other things strewn in his path.

Observing a couple of dozen guys go through that chilling process as the line drew me close to the tower, I became more frightened. And suddenly, terror changed to defiance. I began to think, "I don't have to jump off that thing. I can refuse on the ground that I'm too young to be in the Navy." But, then, what would happen to Babe? Wouldn't she be in trouble? Those sobering questions caused me to see that I had no choice but to take on the monster.

When my turn came to climb the ladder, I stopped thinking about my fears and faced my moment of truth. I began carefully and steadily climbing the steps to the top, always looking up. Even when reaching the top, and while listening to the proctor's nstructions, I refused to look down at the water and kept my eyes glued to the ceiling of the building.

The proctor said, "I want you to cross your arms, put one hand under your chin and cradle it between your thumb and index finger. Make a gap between your thumb and fingers of your other hand and place the gap under your armpit and hold it there." He demonstrated what he said and told me to do the same. I precisely followed his instruction as he watched closely. Then he said, "I want you to walk to the edge of the platform and when I say jump—jump." Looking up at the ceiling, I stood at the edge of the platform fully dressed with my hands positioned as instructed, with no thought in my head other than "Don't look down." Suddenly the proctor tapped me on the back and said, "Jump!"

With my body tense and straight as an arrow, and without the slightest hesitation, I closed my eyes and jumped, hitting the water like a dart and feeling as though I was descending to the bottom of the pool. Finally, I stopped going down and attempted my ascent. On the way up, I felt a hand tugging on my leg and gave it a hard kick. The kick broke the hold and enabled me to make it to the surface but with my head poking through the netting at the bottom of a raft. The proctor sitting there gently pushed my head back into the water, causing me to swim completely under it. After emerging, I swam around the other things floating between me and pool side. Finally I reached the side of the pool, pulled myself out, and sat on a bench exhausted but jubilant. I had done it!

I told a guy, who had jumped ahead of me, about the boot grabbing my leg. He said it had to be the same guy he saw being pulled to the side of the pool. Whenever a guy jumped from the tower and couldn't swim nonstop around each of the obstacles in the water, proctors helped him out of the pool by extending a long pole for him to grab. As soon as the hapless boot grabbed the pole at its tip end, he was pulled to the side of the pool and left to climb out. That whole "rescue" scene was kind of funny to watch, especially if you'd passed the test.

The guy who tugged at my leg had taken swimming lessons as a nonqualified swimmer (NQS) and hadn't done well. Yet he wanted to be tested anyway because he couldn't finish boot training otherwise. Scuttlebutt was that when the proctor at the top of the tower said, "Jump," the NQS hesitated and the proctor gave him a nudge. I felt sorry for him because he had to remain in boot camp and go through the tower thing again until he could pass the test.

After ten weeks on the bluff above the Susquehanna River in Bainbridge, I finished boot camp, was given a promotion and, in my mind, became a real sailor.

Following completion of boot camp training, our company was given a nine-day leave before being ordered to active duty. During this time and while still in Bainbridge, I wanted to see what nearby Baltimore and Philadelphia were like. One afternoon I tagged along with a couple of guys to Baltimore. There, in a bar, the launching of my career as a bona fide sailor was a disgrace.

Dressed in our blues and looking every bit like military men, we went into a bar and ordered drinks. The bartender looked me in the face and said, "Let me see your I.D.," catching me completely by surprise. I said, "I.D., don't you see my uniform? I'm in the Navy." He said, "Sorry, but it's the law. You gotta be 21." What he really meant was you have to look 21. He didn't ask my buddies, who weren't 21, to see their I.D. because they looked 21 to him. Try as I might, there was no way I could look 21. Being unable to drink with the guys cramped my style. What a drag! Of course when we returned to Bainbridge, the word went out that I was a sailor who couldn't buy a drink. Guys kidded me about it until I was transferred out.

On my next liberty, I went alone to Philadephia—about 60 miles east of Bainbridge. There, I rode a subway train for the first time, sitting next to a friendly teenage girl who gave me information about the trains. She had a nice cafe au lait complexion and was tall and slender. She asked me if I'd like to go to a dance, and thinking she was inviting me, I was thrilled. She told me about a dance hall where Lionel Hampton was playing that night. When I asked her where we should meet to go to the dance, she said she couldn't go because she wasn't allowed to stay out that late. Well, that answer sure caught me by surprise. But I was cool. When her stop came, she got up to leave, telling me to go to the dance. I decided to do just that and managed to find my way there. Hamp swung throughout the night doing about 10 minutes on his big recording hit, "Hey Ba Ba Re Bop," and drove the crowd wild.

Back in Bainbridge, there was a fascinating 20-year-old guy, Carlos, from New York City. His skin color was a darker brown than mine, and his features were similar to mine. In short, he looked like an ordinary colored guy with a heritage rooted in the American South. But he wasn't. His native language was Spanish, and he was born in Puerto Rico. "I'm *Puertorriqueno,*" he said repeatedly to guys in the barracks who ribbed him by saying, "You're Negro, like us. And in the white man's eyes, you're just another nigger." Thinking Carlos was trying to say he was different and better than Negroes, they enjoyed taunting him. I had trouble myself understanding how a guy with skin darker than mine could see himself as anything other than a Negro, no matter where he came from. I wanted to know more about him. So when he invited me to hang out with him at his mom's place for a few days in New York City, I leaped at the opportunity.

On the train to New York, I tried hard to curb my excitement and be cool. It was mind-blowing to be on my way to the city Ted Collins had made sound so magical. The train pulled into Penn Station on a cold and snowy day. The station was huge and crowded with people coming and going at a fast pace. Carlos fell right in with it, slowing only to get me to keep up. He wanted to stop at Macy's to pick up a gift for his mom, and so we walked along 33rd. Street to get there.

The shops, people, restaurants, and bars on the way were brimming with people. Macy's was the biggest department store I ever saw. And the sales people were courteous.

After leaving Macy's, we boarded a subway train for Spanish Harlem, transferring once before we got there. The subway wasn't new to me because I rode one in Philadelphia. Yet the ride to Harlem was unlike any subway experience I ever had. Many of the riders looked like ordinary colored folk in the Midwest and South, but like Carlos, they weren't, and they spoke to one another in a language other than English. I asked Carlos who they were. They were either Puerto Ricans, Cubans, Dominicans, Haitians, Panamanians or Africans, I learned. Being from the Midwest, I had no awareness of them. These folk, who were so familiar yet so different, were intriguing to me.

When we got off the train at 110th. Street and Lenox Avenue, I wasn't ready for what I saw. The streets nearby were littered with empty food containers, bits of newspapers, and wine bottles. Piles of dirty snow lined the curbside and the sidewalks were strewn with overfilled garbage cans. While none of this squalor was what I expected to see, I wasn't shocked by it, for it was like home in Mill Creek.

Carlos's mother, Mrs. Guzman, and his brother and family lived on the first floor of a five-story walk-up in a 5-room apartment with two bedrooms and a corridor connecting the rooms. Carlos and I slept on the sofas in the living room. Mrs.Guzman was a short, thin, graying woman with light-brown skin. Her son Luis, age 25, was light-skinned like his wife Alicia, age 21, and baby Jilcia. Except for Jilcia, they were all born in Puerto Rico and spoke both English and Spanish. Mrs. Guzman worked nearby in a bodega and Luis was a musician.

Eager to make the most of our short visit, in addition to sightseeing, I wanted to meet Uncle Jimmy, Mama's brother. He'd been living in New York for nearly 20 years and working as a Pullman Porter, running between Chicago and New York City. But first, I had to see Times Square. So off we went. Boy, what a spectacle of neon lights everywhere—on marquees, cafeterias, arcades and small shops. People of every description were there in a steady stream. It was so easy to get caught up in the sights, sounds and smells of the area. We spent the night at the movies watching triple features, eating popcorn and falling asleep. After waking up, we left one theater and walked next door to another and started the whole thing all over again until we had our fill by dawn and headed for home.

Like Times Square, the Automat was a must see. I'd heard a lot about it and told Carlos I wanted to go there. So he took me to one on East Forty-Second Street near Grand Central Station. After entering, we headed to the cashier where we got a bunch of nickles. Then we went before a huge glass enclosure subdivided into slots of enticing hot and cold food dishes. Each slot had a glass door and all it took was the right number of nickles—one for a cup of coffee, two for baked beans or macaroni and cheese, three for an egg salad sandwich—to open the doors of your choice. You were in full control. You didn't even have to talk to anybody. All you needed was a handful of nickles, to open doors to culinary pleasure.

And, as if that wasn't enough, there was more to the Automat than the magic of a nickle. Its social scene was as engaging and fascinating as its food choices. People of diverse descriptions were there, and they weren't all merely eating. Some were seated at a table either chatting (in a foreign language), playing chess or reading, while making fashion statements with their huge moustaches, shaggy beards, unusual hairstyles and clothing.

Carlos said his brother, Luis, was a timbale player. "What's a timbale?" I asked, having never heard the word before. He said it was like a drum, a kettle-drum. I wasn't sure of what a kettledrum was either. He said Luis loved to talk about his timbales, and I could ask him about them when he came home. Later that evening I chatted with Luis, mentioning that I wanted to know more about what Carlos called "Latin Sounds."

The next night, Carlos went out with his girl, and I went up to the Bronx with Luis who had a gig in a Latin social club. There, I got a chance to see his timbales and to hear him play. The dancers were on the floor as soon as the band kicked off with the first number. Chicks with shapely bodies reacted sexily to the groovy rhythms. They were having so much fun and looking so inviting that I felt like dancing too, but I only looked and listened, not having the courage to try it. This was a very different scene from that in Philadelphia with Lionel Hampton's band. The music and dancers were different; the people were more varied—like the ones on the Harlem bound subway. At that dance in Philadelphia, young women didn't look as appealing dancing the jitterbug as Latin women did dancing the mambo. Both were very expressive doing their thing, but, to me, the subtle and rhythmic movement of hips to the mambo was sexier than the gyrating hip movements to the jitterbug.

Back home in St. Louis at the Castle Ballroom, there was a sexy dance of a different kind. And you saw it whenever dancers fell under the spell of a slow funky blues, like "In the Dark, In the Dark," by Lil Green. Then, you'd see dancers hermetically close and grinding on a dime.

When Luis came off the bandstand, I excitedly told him how much I enjoyed everything—his timbale playing, the music and dance. I tried to talk about the different feeling I got from his music and that of black America, but the words didn't come out right. Yet he knew what I was trying to say and pointed out that while African rhythmic patterns were a part of both musical traditions, it was the Afro-Cuban rhythms that made the big difference between them. He said these rhythms had shaped much of the popular music and dance of Latin America. He invited me to come with him and Alicia to a dance the next night at nearby Park Palace, saying the band there would show me what he was talking about. An Afro-Cuban named Machito would be there with his Afro-Cuban band playing Latin jazz and mambo, he said. I went, got an earful and fell in love with the music and the people.

New York City was everything I imagined it to be—a place of wonder, magic and enchantment. I was amazed by its diverse people. More than once while there, I thought to myself, "This is like many foreign countries all rolled into one."

On my last morning in New York City, I stayed on the sofa unwilling to get up just yet, as my mind skipped from one thought to another. It was incredible how people whom I never thought about before had come racing into my consciousness.

8

Real Sailor

Finally, we got our orders, on a bittersweet day in March, 1946. My buddies, Earl and Carlos, were ordered to the West Coast, and I was sent to Boston. That was the last time I saw either of them.

At 15, I arrived in Boston confident and ready to practice being a sailor. After a week at the Receiving Station, I was assigned to a ship—sort of. My days were spent aboard it and my nights were in the barracks. The ship wasn't going beyond the dock at the South Boston Navy yard, for it had seen its day and was now undergoing the decommissioning process. I was a member of her skeleton crew.

From the barracks, I'd catch a ride to the dock to board the ship, *U.S.S.Kadashan Bay*. Along the way I could see other ships that were sea bound. Taking in these sights made me feel more like a sailor than ever before. Excited, I felt good about my chances of boarding a sea-going ship soon.

Duty aboard the aircraft carrier *Kadashan Bay* was only caretaking. There were no officers aboard so the distinction between seamen's and steward mates' duties was irrelevant. That was cool because it gave me a chance to hang out with seamen and see what they were like.

Full of seafaring tales to lay on a green sailor, they regaled me with many stories, including the history of the *Kadashan Bay*. According to them, the carrier paid some heavy dues during the war. "About a year and a half ago," one guy said, "she took part in the great naval battle that helped McArthur return to the Philippines." Stomping on the deck for emphasis, another guy added, "In Leyte Gulf, planes took off from this very flight deck where we're sitting and attacked them fucking Jap ships!" Seeing how attentive I was, he continued, "During that same battle, a Kamikaze slammed into her amidships." The more they talked about her the more pride I felt to be even a member of her skeleton crew. And when they said she was going to be scrapped, it just didn't seem right.

I had liberty every afternoon and went sightseeing a lot. One day I wandered onto the Boston Common and discovered the Crispus Attucks Monument named after the black-American revolutionary. On Beacon Street, I saw a statue of the 54th. Massachusetts Volunteers, a regiment of all black soldiers who led the charge against the rebel-held Fort Wagner during the Civil War. These discoveries gave me a wonderful impression of Boston, making it seem like a special place.

One morning in the mess hall, I met a steward mate named John, a tall muscular guy about 25, with dark brown skin and weighing about 200 pounds. As we chatted over our clumps of scrambled eggs, I learned he was from Atlanta, stayed in the barracks and was hoping to get duty aboard a sea-going ship. "Where do you hang out?" he asked. I told him I spent my time sightseeing in Boston. "Sightseeing," he said, with contempt, "man that ain't hitting on shit. That's a waste of time. Roxbury is where the action is. That's where you should hang out. You can pick up some fine chicks in the bars." Roxbury sounded like my kind of place. But the memory of the I.D. thing at that bar in Baltimore was still fresh in my mind, and I didn't want to go through that again.

Still if I hadn't been so self-conscious about my lean 15-year-old body, I would have found a way around the I.D. problem. My eagerness to pick up women—like a sailor was expected to do—was incentive enough. But my uniform, drooping from my body like a flag on a flagpole, was a major stumbling block.

So instead of hanging out with John and chasing chicks on the hip bar scene and risking hassles with bartenders, I chose the genteel ladies of a USO club. The women there were always welcoming and friendly, and neither your age nor how you looked in uniform mattered. This was the ideal setting for me until I could gain some experience in socializing with other types of full-grown women. Each guy in the club had a shot at the attention of every hostess there. The club's mission was to entertain servicemen and make them "feel at home away from home." No booze or hanky-panky with the women was allowed. You could look but you better not touch. The ages of the women seemed to range from the early 20's to the early 30's. It was great talking to them, although some of the older ones tended to talk down to me. One of the younger ones—whom I would have loved to date—was sweet and a terrific dancer. Merely chatting with her from time to time was a great confidence builder and caused me to be much less self-conscious.

One morning at breakfast, I mentioned to John how much I liked going to the USO. Looking sneeringly at me, he said, "Man, you ain't gonna get no pussy there. That place is for squares. You better let me turn you on to what's happening in Roxbury." After hearing this over and over again whenever I ran into him at breakfast, I went to Roxbury with him one afternoon. Avoiding the bars or cabarets as they were called then, I hung out in a poolroom. In this area along Columbus Avenue, it could get a little rowdy at times, and it was good to be associated with John because he knew what was going on. And being a big tough cat, he was respected.

One night John came into the poolroom where I was shooting pool and said to me, "Finish up and come on. I'll buy you a drink." Believing I'd be hassled by the bartender about my age, I turned him down. But he insisted, saying "Ah, come on. What's the problem?" I was embarrassed to tell him about me and bartenders. His insistence, however, caused me to say that I was sure I'd be asked for my I.D. John said, "That I.D. don't mean shit. You're in the Navy ain't you; that's all that counts. Come on let's go." He was so sure of himself that I went along with him. At the bar, after asking me if I wanted a beer, John ordered two. While the bartender poured the beer, John introduced me as his friend. From that time on, thanks to the regard the bartender had for my overbearing buddy, I could order whatever I wanted without having to show I.D.

Often going there without John, I became a regular. It was fun checking out the different people in the bar. Once I watched a guy pick up a chick by sending her a drink and waiting for her to give him the okay before moving on her. I thought that was cool.

One night when I was in the bar doing my thing, the finest chick in the world walked in, sat at the bar a few stools away and smiled at me. Encouraged and excited, I moved over next to her and said, "May I buy you a drink?" She gave me the sweetest smile and said, "Yes, thank you." She was gorgeous—about 21, 5 feet, seven inches tall, 125 curvacious pounds and shoulder length wavy hair. Her make-up was light and becoming. She wore a simple plain dress, low-heel shoes and spoke with a quiet soothing voice. There was nothing about her appearance or manner to suggest she wanted anything other than company. While she was the sexiest woman I ever met, it wasn't her sex appeal alone that took center stage. It was also her simplicity and charm that made her so likeable. "Where are you from?" she asked.

"I'm from St. Louis," I said, "and I've been in Boston only a short time. Are you a Bostonian?"

"No, I'm from Leominster," she said.

I wasn't sure if she was colored or white and hoped she'd say something to settle the question. "Do you like Boston?" I asked.

"I don't know yet, but I'm trying to," she said after a slight hesitation. "I came to Boston hoping to find a good job. And I'm still looking."

I was thrilled by the attention she was giving me and suggested we move from the bar to a table. A few minutes after we sat down and I was feeling completely at ease, John walked in, noticed us, and immediately walked toward our table. As he approached, I quickly told her my name and learned hers was Samantha. Without being invited to join us, John sat down as I knew he would. Facing them both, I said, "Samantha this is my friend John, and John this is Samantha." I was uncomfortable with the feeling that John, and his jive manner, was going to mess up the nice groove Samantha and I had going. As he settled in, I sat nervously. He ogled her without regard for me. And I read his thoughts, "Who was she? And what was she doing with me?" He went to get a drink and quickly returned to the table. He couldn't keep his eyes off her. "Janet's coming any minute now, and we can all hang out," he said. "Oh, who's Janet?" I asked. "Don't you remember?" he asked. "I told you about her."

Minutes later, a short, brown-skinned, chubby chick about John's age wiggled over to our table smiling. She greeted John as he pulled out a chair, motioned to her to sit down and then made the introductions. John had told me a few days ago about a chick he met. "She ain't nothin to look at but she's got some good pussy," he said. So I figured Janet was the one.

John quickly became the center of attention, telling one dirty joke after another, causing Janet to howl. To my surprise Samantha wasn't at all offended but was laughing too and joining Janet in encouraging him to keep it up. Time went by, drinks went down, jokes got nastier and laughter got louder. John had a talent for telling jokes. I liked them, but I had put Samantha on a pedestal and saw the jokes as too vile for her ears, despite her laughter—which I wanted to believe was merely her way of being polite. When the laughter died down for an instant, John said, "Let's split this scene and move our party to Beulah's." Beulah was the name of a woman who rented rooms by the hour in her rooming house. I knew that but didn't think Samantha did. "Great idea!" I said. "Let's go." Samantha surprised me with her tacit and unquestioning consent. We then left the bar, bought a bottle of scotch, soda and cups and went to Beulah's for a room.

By then I'd drunk three beers, and instead of feeling mellow, I felt jittery and kind of nervous as we settled into the room. Things were happening too fast for me. Within fewer than five minutes, John and Janet were sitting on one side of the bed sipping their drinks and noisily kissing. As I poured Samantha a drink, I stole a glance at John's hand probing the dark recesses under Janet's skirt as she squirmed. I sensed Samantha was in the mood to mess around too. But I wasn't.

There was no way for me to move on this gorgeous woman with other people in the room. Still, I went through the motions, by taking her hand, leading her to the other side of the bed, drawing her into my arms and kissing her. To my surprise, she responded passionately, and so I eagerly started to probe beneath her dress, caressing her thighs with my hot hand moving slowly upward.

Meanwhile, John and Janet were about to really get it on, stripping off their clothes and tossing them on the floor. Their intrusion upon our side of the bed caused me to stop, take Samantha by the hand and move away from the bed. "Whatcha moving for? The bed's big enuff for y'all too," John murmured. Not trusting him to keep his hands away from Samantha, I kept her on the edge of the bed out of his reach. Wailing in orgasmic delight, John and Janet signaled that the end was near. And minutes later, they dressed and left the room.

Yet, despite being alone with this fantastic woman, the thrill was gone, and I was unable to rise to the occasion. Baffled and mortified, I couldn't believe what was happening—or not happening. This was the ideal woman and the perfect moment for my sexual rite of passage. So how could this be happening to me, I achingly wondered. Samantha had to have been surprised by this disappointing outcome too, but she took it calmly without expressing displeasure. As we dressed and left Beulah's, I was sure she didn't want to see me again. We said goodbye on the street, and I returned by taxi to the barracks. It was kind of funny how the evening had been full of surprises—Samantha's behavior didn't jibe with the image I had of her, and I was sure mine didn't fit the one she had of me.

I ran into John in the mess hall the next day. "Man, where did you get that fine chick? She's built like a brick shit house," he said. I told him I'd only met her an hour or so before he came into the bar. I hoped he wouldn't ask me what it was like to have sex with her. But he did. Smirking, he said, "I bet that bitch got some good pussy." I said, "It was great," and left it at that. I wasn't about to tell him what had really happened.

About a week later, John told me he ran into Samantha and they had sex. He was beside himself with satisfaction, wanting to fill me in with all the details. Anxious to know if she'd told him about my inability to get an erection, I listened, expecting him to say she had. But it didn't happen and I was relieved. Yet I was unhappy to learn that Samantha whom I still wanted to think of as a sweet innocent young woman, down on her luck, could be picked up by a guy like John.

A few days later, I found John waiting for me at breakfast. Before I could get started on my eggs, he said at short arm inspection, they told him he had clap. This was a rare moment to see him so riled up. He was completely mystified, saying Samantha was the last woman he'd been with. Looking straight at me, he said, "You don't have clap. Do you?"

   "No," I said, why should I?"

9

The Andy

On June 26, 1946, my dream of going to sea was about to be realized. That was the day I was assigned to duty aboard a troop transport, the *U.S.S. General A.E. Anderson* a.k.a. the Andy. The word from veteran steward mates among the crew was that she was very special, having transported thousands of combat troops around the world during the war. She was in dry dock when I boarded her in the South Boston Navy Yard. The Andy was my cave, promising enrichment—like that of Ali Baba and his forty thieves.

Now that the war was over, according to the steward mates, the mission of the Andy was no longer exclusively that of moving troops around the world. It now included transporting dependents of servicemen—wives and children—to and from overseas ports as cabin-class passengers. In dry dock, her amidships had been altered to create accommodations for them, with spacious staterooms, ample medical support, a nursery and lounges—all in one area known as cabin country.

The Andy was a humongous ship with a glorious history. The word was that she had been in dry dock since coming up from Norfolk, Virginia in April. Before then, she had ferried troops and supplies to Europe, North Africa, and Asia during the war, having made 28 crossings of the Atlantic, 6 of the Indian Ocean, and 8 of the Pacific. She could carry as many as 5000 troops in addition to 500 officers and enlisted men. Her 2 engine rooms kept her moving. There were 2 cargo cranes and 5 cargo holds capable of holding 2700 tons of equipment and supplies. And she could protect herself with her 4 cannons, 4 twin 40 milimeter aircraft mounts, and 18 twin 20 milimeter mounts.

Andy's steward mates catered not only to her officers' lodging and food needs but to the similar needs of the cabin-class passengers as well. The dependents kept to themselves in cabin country, secluded from the crew, troops and Seabees. Only steward mates and other authorized personnel were allowed in cabin country. Authorized personnel included servicemen traveling with their families. They were allowed to visit in cabin country with their wives and children until taps. Marines were stationed at the entrance to enforce the seclusion rule.

Steward mates had their own compartment, separate and apart from the white crew members. Within our compartment, we had our own head, bunks, and lockers. It took a while for me to get used to living in the cold-raw-steel environment of the ship. Steel was everywhere—under my feet, above my head, the bulkheads to the right and left, the frame of my bunk, my locker—it was like living in a house of steel, but I soon got used to it.

Some of the guys' bunks were gathering places like street corners in a black neighborhood, with guys hanging out there telling whoppers about their sexual exploits in Roxbury and elsewhere, playing the dozens and running the tale of the signifying monkey. Except for a few Filipinos, we were all black, and many of us were newly assigned to the ship and looked forward to shoving off on our first sea voyage.

There was little contact between black and white sailors, although there were no rules against it. Whether black and white crew members had anything to do with one another aboard ship or ashore depended upon the racial attitudes they brought with them to the Navy. An Italian guy from Brooklyn, Tony, would come into our compartment, whenever he ran out of something to put on his hair, yelling, "Anybody got any grease?" He and Joe, a steward mate from Brooklyn, were buddies, and they were known as "jitterbug kings" at a dance hall in Roxbury. While some white guys chose to have nothing to do with steward mates for whatever reason, there were also some who were simply indifferent. The same can be said of steward mates in respect to white crew members. However, the color line was always ignored for an opportunity to make a few dollars at some of the crap games and poker games in our compartment. Then, black and white sailors got together and were equally free—to woo lady luck.

The first few days aboard the Andy, I was so caught up in her that I stayed on board rather than go ashore on liberty. I liked the idea that the Andy was both the place I lived and worked and that I could meet a lot of my needs without ever leaving her. It was fun locating the post office, PX, gym, and the place on deck where movies were shown.

On or about July 6, 1946, I anxiously went topsides to watch us cast off and put out to sea for Norfolk. As we made our way through Boston Harbor to the Atlantic Ocean, I felt great and laughed off teasing from some steward mates about seasickness. But after about an hour on the Atlantic, I slowly began to feel so bad that nothing in life seemed to matter. I had discovered the horrors of seasickness. When the guys graphically described "real turbulence" and said that they saw no reason for me to be sick on the "calm Atlantic," I thought they were heartless. Their trash talk had the desired effect, causing me to vomit more and feel completely hopeless. To get away from those jive cats, I went topsides for fresh air. Stumbling and holding on to the hand rails, I reached a bench, plopped on it and slowly stretched out. As I lay there ruing the day I joined the Navy, I agonizingly emptied my guts and remained sick until we reached Norfolk.

After an overnight stop, we shoved off and returned to the Atlantic. By then, I'd learned a lesson from my former tormentors about seasickness that I was ready to put into practice: eat three squares, stay busy and avoid the bow of the ship.

We were underway for only a few hours when I heard we were on our way to San Francisco with a stop at Colon before going through the Panama Canal. This was thrilling news, and I checked out the route on an atlas to appreciate it fully. I poured over the map, tracing the path of the voyage into the Caribbean to Panama, to the Pacific and up the long coast of Central America to California. It was the stuff dreams were made of, and I was ecstatic.

My buddy, Bill—a 20-year-old, tall, olive-skinned, curly head guy from Georgia—and I went ashore on liberty in Colon. The red-light district was off-limits to all sailors, due to an understanding reached by the civilian and military authorities. According to the scuttlebutt, prior to the arrival of the Andy, some sailors had wrecked the district over a dispute involving some senoritas and pimps. It didn't matter to me because I wanted to take a closer look at the people of Panama. Bill and I strolled the streets of a poor section of town, checking out the scene. The local people who smiled and waved at us reminded me of people I'd seen in Spanish Harlem.

The most fun in Colon took place in a run-down bar where we stopped for a cool drink. There, I spotted a beat-up-lopsided piano in a corner and sat down at it to pick out a few bars of boogie-woogie music. To my surprise, it drew the attention of a small group of people who quickly gathered about the piano expecting to hear much more music than I could play. We had so much fun that I left there promising myself to take piano lessons someday.

July 24, 1946, was a very special day. Before noon, as I stood topsides looking at the horizon, I spotted land on our approach to San Francisco Bay, and wanted to be up on deck to watch it all. As I stood near the railing among a small group of guys, I listened and looked, as they talked like tour guides, and knew we were entering the bay under the Golden Gate Bridge, and that we were close enough to Alcatraz to sense life on it. With the help of tug boats, the Andy made her way to one of the many piers located under the San Francisco-Oakland Bay Bridge. The exciting Bay Area with its picturesque scenes was an excellent introduction to San Francisco. I was convinced that the sailor who said, "Frisco is one of the best liberty ports in the world" was right on the money. I couldn't wait to go ashore.

I'll never forget my first liberty in San Francisco. Bill, our buddy Joe and I got into a taxi at the pier, and the driver—aware that our ship had just come in—said, "I bet I know where you guys wanna go. Where the girls are. Right?"

"Yeah," we answered, "Right!" Chatting all the way, the driver soon pulled up in front of a building with two or three young beauties hanging out of the windows, smiling and waving at us.

"This is the place," he said with a sly grin.

As we climbed the steps to the front door, a smiling fortyish-looking white woman standing at the top greeted us. We all smiled at her, and Joe said, "We came to have a good time." She said, "Good, you came to the right place." Joe was 23 and acted as though he had been to a cathouse before. He was so cool. I wanted to act like him, but I was too nervous and excited. It was unimaginable to be in a place with stunning chicks ready to give me pleasure without a care about my appearance and inexperience—a place where I could let my money talk the talk.

As we were led to a spacious room with deep-cushioned chairs, couches and a bar, I was captivated. Our hostess said, "Why don't you order a drink while I bring the girls out." We stood at the bar, and I ordered a beer hoping it would settle me down. A few minutes later, our hostess returned with six dazzling young ladies wearing spike heels and transparent gowns above the knees. They stood in a line before us as our hostess introduced them by first name, and on cue, each one revealed a gloriously sexy body as she opened her gown. At this point, I was beside myself with lust and ordered something stronger than beer in order to calm down. These bewitching ladies, lined up before us, ran the gamut—black, white, Asian and various combinations in between. They were a mosaic of skin color, hair color and texture, facial features, height, and curves. And not a single one weighed over 130 pounds or looked to be over 22 years old.

Our hostess invited us to "choose a partner." Still shook up by the whole thing, I kept sipping scotch, trying to be cool as my fantasies appeared before me in living color. Without paying any attention to me, Bill and Joe quickly chose a playmate and disappeared. Before I knew it, a lovely Eurasian girl, sensing my confused state, sashayed over to me, took my hand and led me to a private room. It was then and there that I learned the joys of sex and lost my innocence.

After several days of taking on passengers for its maiden voyage, the Andy began its rotating voyages to the Far East, with San Francisco as our home port.

It was amazing how things were turning out exactly the way I envisioned. I was about to see the world of the Pacific and East Asia. In August, 1946, we put out to sea headed for Hawaii, our first port of call.

When we sailed into Pearl Harbor, I was topsides taking in the sights, while the ship's loudspeakers blared the Hawaian music piped in from the radio. As I stood looking over the harbor, I recalled that Sunday, December 7, 1941, when I'd just left the Comet Theater and heard somebody on the street yell, "The Japs bombed Pearl Harbor!" I thought, "How amazing it was for me to be in this harbor fewer than 5 years afterwards."

Bill, Joe and I went on liberty in Honolulu expecting to have a good time, despite the talk about it not being friendly to black sailors. We tried to ignore the rumor and went about our sightseeing, hoping we'd find some chicks to hang out with. As far as we could tell, there wasn't a whorehouse there. However, there was a bar in Honolulu said to be a great place to pick up a chick, but the word was that its white owner and the white sailors who hung out there had declared it off-limits to colored soldiers and sailors. Joe, being of a different mind, said, "Let's check it out." Bill said, "I don't wanna go where I'm not welcome." They both looked at me, wanting to know what I thought. I agreed with Bill and said, "Let's pass it up." And so we did.

Because Bill looked sort of Hawaiian and Joe was a young Muhammad Ali look-alike—handsome, tall and over 200 pounds—I thought we looked good enough to pick up some Hawaiian beauties on the beach or even on the street. Bill and Joe looked great in their uniforms, and women were drawn to them—except in Honolulu.

Although Honolulu was not a good liberty town, it was an interesting one. There, I saw a volcano for the first time in my life. Also, it was a treat to spend a few hours on beautiful Waikiki Beach which had it all over the beaches along Lake Michigan. But the biggest bang in Honolulu came from a tattoo parlor where the artist created an image of a small bird perched on a limb that spelled "mother," on my forearm. A tattoo, according to the lore of sailors, was 1 of the 3 criteria to be met in order to become a genuine salt.

One night, we drank too much and were approached by Shore Patrol (SP) as we walked noisily along the pier back to the Andy. "Pipe down! You're making too goddamn much noise," one of them yelled. We said nothing and kept on our merry way. The two SP guys then stopped us a few steps before we reached our gangplank and warned us again. At that point, Joe yelled, "Shove off." But they had other ideas and didn't leave. Instead, they rushed ahead of us right up the gangplank and reported us to the deck officer, charging us with unruly conduct and disrespect. The officer wrote up the charges against us as stated by the SP. Those charges led to a Captain's Mast, a judicial hearing conducted by the executive officer (exec). At the hearing, the exec said we should choose a single speaker from among us to address the charges. Bill and Joe looked at me signifying they wanted me to speak. I then admitted we were noisy but had lowered the noise level after being told to do so. Furthermore, I said that when the SP followed us along the pier to our gangplank, we felt that we were being picked on.

The exec was unmoved by our defense and assigned us extra duty—which meant for seven nights, we had to clean the scullery. He scornfully added, "You must make it immaculate" and then asked if we knew what "immaculate" meant. None of us did. He had exposed our lack of knowledge in a manner that was more punishing to me than the extra duty penalty. I resented his assumption about our ignorance and felt ashamed that I'd never heard of the word. I vowed from then on to expand my vocabulary and started by finding a dictionary and looking up the meaning of immaculate.

Two weeks after leaving Pearl Harbor, we sailed into Tokyo Bay. While taking in the sights and sounds on deck, I thought to myself, "So this is Japan. What a sad place. Everything is so gloomy and dark." I had mixed feelings about the Japanese. On the one hand I was happy we socked it to them, but later when I walked the streets of Tokyo and saw the wretchedness of the place and its people, I felt sympathy for them.

As I strolled on the dimly lit streets, I noticed people trudging along with heads bowed and faces expressionless. In the shops, though merchants were eager to get U.S. dollars from us, they paid us little attention as we browsed. And when we made a purchase, they accepted payment in a robotic fashion. The artists on the streets painting sailors' portraits on silk hankerchiefs were mechanical too. And while sitting for one artist, I noticed he had scarcely given me a sign of welcome, even after beckoning me to sit for a portrait.

Except for the purchase of a Japanese camera, which was aided nicely by an unbelievable foreign exchange rate, my experiences in Tokyo were totally lacking in fun. The camera turned out to be a great source of pleasure, for I was able to shoot some precious pictures in the Far East.

After a day or two in Tokyo we made an overnight stop down the Bay at Yokosuka, which had been the site of one of Japan's major naval bases. Under the complete control of the United States, it was regarded as important to U.S. operations in Japan. There was nothing memorable about Yokosuka except for an enormous crane along the pier where the Andy docked. There was no liberty and no regrets.

From Tokyo Bay, we steamed into the East China Sea and on to Tsingtao. I stopped thinking about seeing China's Great Wall when I learned that it was too far north. Throughout our stay there, a pungent odor filled the air. I was shocked to hear that the odor was caused by human fertilizer. I didn't know whether it was true or not, but I hoped it wasn't. Since the Chinese had been on our side, I felt friendly toward them and looked forward to checking them out.

Tsingtao was a big city and its streets were bustling with people. Men carried large sacks of rice on the back of bicycles along broad streets. It was fun taking in the sights from the vantage point of a rickshaw.

Like taxi drivers in the States, rickshaw men were wonderful sources of information, and they knew where the girls were. After a brief meeting of the minds with one of them, Bill, Joe and I—in three separate rickshaws—were carried to a huge housing complex which consisted of horseshoe shaped 3 story buildings. There, in families of 3 or 4 generations, more than a half dozen people lived in 4 or 5 room apartments. Striking seductive poses, pretty girls who appeared to be in their late teens and early twenties paraded in front of their apartments. The guys and I were amazed by what was going on because we could see people in the girls' apartments doing ordinary things like cooking, sitting around and talking to each other. In other words, while mama was cooking and papa was talking to grandpapa, daughter was out front trying to lure a trick. We saw this scene repeated throughout the complex as we strolled from floor to floor.

Bill, Joe and I split up to pursue our respective dream girl. I spotted a girl who appeared to be about 18 or 19 and walked over to her and smiled. She returned the smile and motioned for me to enter the apartment. I did, and found a man who may have been her grandfather. Speaking only a few words of English, the girl gestured and pointed to the old man indicating that the proceedings began with him. Slightly grinning, I took a few dollars from my wallet and handed it to him. With a nod, he accepted them and ushered me and the girl into an empty back room. Alone together, we smiled at each other and she undressed. As I fondled her, I felt lust rapidly transforming into embarrassment. She was far from full grown and seemed even younger than I. Her breasts were underdeveloped, and her hymen was still in place. Despite her protest, I put my clothes on, took her hand, put a dollar in it, and left to look for Bill and Joe.

We sailed out of Tsingtao with some passengers bound for the States. Among them were 3 Chinese whom I found particularly interesting. Two were cadets in the air force of Nationalist China. Often meeting on deck, we chatted about life in China and the United States. They were excited about going to Texas for pilot training. I took their picture with my Japanese camera.

The other Chinese was a tall, beautiful and curvacious young woman, the daughter of an important government official on her way to college in the States. A young American Marine officer, who also boarded the ship in Tsingtao, was apparently smitten by her and was her constant dining companion. Disregarding rules which forbade close contact between unmarried passengers, he attempted to visit her in cabin country, but was stopped at the entrance and reported.

Bill and I were primarily assigned to the passenger dining room, and Joe worked in cabin country. We would trade stories with each other about what was happening in the two areas. Normally, little happened in the dining room worthy of telling. However, there was one event and its consequences that was the talk of the steward mates. One day, enroute to Okinawa, I was waiting tables and had stacked dishes on a nearby stand after clearing them from tables. Suddenly the stand toppled over onto the deck. It was a disaster, and just about everything was broken. Discounting my explanation that it was an accident caused by the turbulent sea, the steward (a petty officer) standing amid the breakage, accused me of "shirking duty" and "insolence to a petty officer." His charges led to a Captain's Mast.

On September 26, 1946, at the Captain's Mast, the exec accepted the charges of the steward, and to my horror, I was given a Summary Court Martial and placed on indefinite restriction. Fortunately, the officers involved in the decision questioned the severity of their punitive action, and although they maintained it to be a court marshall offense, they eventually reduced it to the lowest level, the Deck Court Marshall.

At the Deck Court Martial, I was tried and sentenced to a reduction in rank and fined a month's pay. The whole thing was so unjust and demoralizing.

As the Andy approached the dock in Okinawa, I looked out at the island and had a profoundly eerie feeling about it. This was the grimmest place I ever saw. It had been a hard fought battle for the United States, and I had deep respect for the Americans who lost their lives to gain it. One day, from dockside, I saw a small work detail of Japanese prisoners marching along the dock in the custody of an armed American soldier. As I watched them pass in formation in front of the Andy, the sight of the colored soldier with his prisoners filled me with pride. Many Japanese soldiers were still hiding in caves, unaware that the war had ended. Our stay in Okinawa was short, and there was no liberty.

After a few days out of Okinawa, we put into Manila Bay enroute to Manila, the city with its well touted ladies. And though still on restriction, and not permitted to go ashore, I was excited to be there and saw as much of it as could be seen from the ship. A few days passed before we sailed the short distance around

Manila Bay to Subic Bay, the home of a huge U.S. Naval Base. While there, the lone Filipino aboard ship, a good buddy steward mate, went ashore to visit his native village. True to his word, he returned with a village confection which he cheerfully handed me. It was an egg treated in some special way with artistic decoration. Rather than eat it, I kept it. And it became symbolic of my voyage to the Philippines.

We left the Philipphines for Guam. There, the skipper didn't grant liberty, but instead permitted the crew—black and white jointly—to have a beer party ashore. Guam didn't excite me, but since I hadn't been ashore since Tsingtao, I decided to join the party. A truck picked us up at the ship's gangplank and took us to an area set aside for recreation. The beer was warm and the weather was hot and humid. After hours of watching a boring softball game and listening to bull, I was anxious to return to the ship.

From the truck on the way back to the ship, a young native woman was sighted searching about for something along the beach. She was about a dozen yards away, when two seamen cried out to her, "Hey Baby!" and "Wait right there!" She looked up at the first cry and then returned to what she was doing. Somebody told the truck driver to slow down. He did, and two guys jumped off the truck and trotted over in the direction of the woman, as the driver resumed his speed and continued onward toward the Andy. I never heard what happened to either the woman or the guys who went after her.

After many days at sea, we were returning to Pearl Harbor and then on to San Francisco. During the voyages, steward mates spent a lot of time writing letters, watching movies, playing cards and shooting craps. I learned to play poker, and it became my favorite game—especially draw poker. It was played with deuces wild and a 5 dollar limit on the bet. A game would start about 8:00 at night and continue beyond taps. Craps, on the other hand, was not my game. Although I learned to shoot craps also, it was too fast for me. Still it was more popular among the guys than poker. It was nothing to find both games going on at the same time. In the head of our compartment we were safe from detection by the Master-at Arms.

One clear and breezy morning while enroute to Pearl Harbor, I went to the gym, as I often did on my off duty days at sea. There were never more than a few people present when I showed up, and I liked it that way. I'd punch the speed bag and hit the heavy bag to my delight without an audience. Soon I learned to punch the speed bag as rhythmically as real boxers. Then I began to think of myself as a fighter and sparred with whoever was available. When I learned that the organizers of a boxing match were looking for some boxers, I was excited and quickly signed up.

I didn't know whom I was going to fight until a few minutes before the bout. But it didn't matter because I felt great and was ready to rumble. I climbed into the ring against a seaman named Bates, a chunky guy about 20 and outweighing me by 20 pounds or more. But the difference in weight didn't matter because I felt strong, having lifted weights in addition to working out with the punching bag. I was confident and eager for the three rounds of boxing.

The first round was no sweat. Bates kept his distance and I had to go after him. I thought he was a little intimidated and tested the notion with a couple of right crosses set up by my everpresent left jab in his face. He backed up throughout the second round, with me peppering him with my left jab and following up with a right cross. By the third round, he hadn't hurt me with anything he'd thrown. Coasting along and assured of victory, I thought I'd won the admiration of the spectators with my boxing skills, until suddenly somebody loudly yelled, "You don't have to hit him Bates. Just let him stand there, and the wind'll blow him away!" That advice got Bates into a lot of trouble, for I went after him and caught him with a stiff right to the face. He grimaced, back pedaled and evaded me for the rest of the round. My performance may not have won the respect of some on-lookers, but, as they say, I "emerged victorious."

No matter what I ate or how often, I couldn't gain weight. And missing a meal would cause me to lose weight. At about 135 pounds and close to 6 feet, my upper body was small and my legs were long and skinny. Despite my muscular development, I didn't have a boxer's body, and as much as I liked boxing, that was my only bout, though I continued to work out in the gym.

A few days before reaching Pearl Harbor, my buddy Joe told me about two guys, Sam and Dave, who worked in cabin country with him. They had been put on report and charged with molesting two women passengers. A steward claimed he had seen Sam holding the hand of a woman in her stateroom. At the same time, her roommate and Dave, according to the same petty officer, were heard laughing and talking together. Sam was a tall, handsome, caramel-skinned, well built, guy from the East Coast, friendly, hip and known to have a way with women. Dave, who was medium height, well built, mahogany-skinned and not bad looking, was regarded as a serious guy who enjoyed conversation. The two women—both young and white—told the complaining petty officer that they'd enjoyed the friendly chats with the two guys and that neither one had ever behaved improperly. Through the grapevine, other steward mates heard about it. And we all wondered how it would turn out.

At the Captain's Mast, Dave said he was only having a friendly chat with the woman and saw nothing wrong with that. He also minced no words in supporting what Sam had said in his own defense. He said Sam was only being friendly to the woman and was not holding her hand but that she was touching his in the course of a conversation. Yet, despite the supporting statements of the two women, Sam was put in the brig and held there until transferred off the ship. Dave was given hours of extra duty in the scullery and restricted to the ship for an indefinite period. I didn't know either of those guys, but I believed they got the shaft.

Many steward mates felt the punishment was harsh and unfair, arguing that by the women's own admission, the men had not forced their attention on them. A few other steward mates, not anxious to discuss the matter, viewed Sam and Dave as reckless and foolish in their behavior, even if the women had welcomed their attention. One steward mate said, "The white man don't want you messing round with his woman, period." I took the punitive action against the two men to be further proof of the little regard for steward mates. And I immediately thought about that marine officer who got off light even though it was clear that he had tried to seduce that young Chinese woman who came aboard at Tsingtao.

In November, 1946, we returned to Pearl Harbor, and I was still unable to go ashore on liberty. But I was comfortable with that because I'd be off restriction by the time we arrived back in our home port.

As we sailed into the Bay Area, it was as if it was my first time seeing it. I stood on deck gazing at the scenic beauty. What a pleasure to be back! After we docked for passengers to disembark, I watched as steward mates carried luggage onto the pier to waiting taxis and other vehicles. Dave, the steward mate accused with Sam of wrongdoing, carried a passenger's bags onto the pier and instead of returning to the ship got into a taxi and took off, jumping ship. "Well I'll be damned," I thought, "He was a pretty cool cat to do that."

10

Living The Dream

I felt great getting my feet back on the ground in San Francisco, the beautiful American city that gave me such pleasure. Wandering alone on Market Street, I enjoyed the feeling of being free to go into restaurants, stores, and movies. One day while on Market, I noticed a huge marquee advertising the Duke Ellington Orchestra at a majestic movie theater. On the spur of the moment, I walked up to the box office and purchased a ticket. And with an exhilarating feeling of welcome, I went in, bought popcorn and enjoyed the show. It was heart-warming to have this feeling of freedom in my home port.

In the Fillmore District, at my favorite house of pleasure, I became chummy with a few of the racially diverse working ladies, learning a lot about them as they talked about their personal lives, goals, and outlook. Apart from what they did for a living, they were like many other young women, and a few of them aspired to eventually do other things, like going to college and getting married and having babies. I liked hanging out there with them.

The Fillmore District evolved from a Japanese neighborhood to a mostly black one during the war. It became a pretty hip place with black-owned businesses, night clubs and bars. I met Julie at one of those bars where she worked as a barmaid—and where I was never hassled for I.D. "Where are you from?" she asked. "How long have you been in the Navy?" I don't think she ever asked me my age. I guessed she figured it was about 19 or 20. Talking to her was like talking to a buddy, I felt free to speak frankly about any subject. I talked about the women in the brothel and how they were nicer than the working girls who approached me on the streets, asking, "Do you want to have a good time?" She warned me, "Be careful about the girls on the street. Some of them are dirty bitches."

Julie was a pretty woman who, unlike other barmaids in Fillmore, was not fancy in her dress or makeup. She had a clear and smooth looking light-brown skinned face that lit up when she was amused. And she seemed always ready to laugh. Her hair was shoulder length and her body, 5 feet, 5 inches, was shapely and a little plump. She had a delightful disposition which I imagined helped her get over the guy who left her high and dry after they'd come to San Francisco from Dallas. I got the impression that Julie had paid some heavy dues.

It wasn't long before our friendship took on a sexual dimension, and I was invited to her pad in the Booker T. Washington Hotel. I learned to like Julie a lot despite my initial feeling that she was too old, at 34. She was the first woman with whom I had an intimate relationship that included friendship. I'd shack up with her on weekend liberty and sometimes over-night. She was good for my self-esteem. She accepted me as I appeared and made me feel she cared. She enjoyed hearing stories about my voyages in the Pacific and Far East and encouraged me to talk about them. Although she never asked me for any money, I knew she was saving money with the intention of returning to Dallas, and so I'd give her something from time to time.

It was great hanging out with her. Occasionally we'd go out to a club. Once she took me to a party in Fillmore where the guy who opened the door handed each of us what I learned later was a reefer. Julie accepted it in a routine manner. But I didn't know what it was, why he gave it to me or what I was expected to do with it. Yet I tried to be cool and not even ask Julie about it. I trailed behind her as she walked through one room after another in the dimly lighted apartment. In one room, I noticed people huddled in small groups, chatting and taking long drags on a reefer. When I turned to say something to Julie, she had already disappeared in the haze.

This was a completely new thing to me. I had no idea who the people were or what was being talked about. Everything was so hushed with people having little or no contact with those outside their group. Julie was sitting and chatting away, having left me to fend for myself. This was a very uncomfortable situation for me. I didn't know what to make of this whole scene—which was not to my liking, including the awful odor of the smoke. The reefer was still in my breast pocket, and I had no intention of smoking it. I gestured to Julie that I wanted to talk to her. She left her group to find out what I wanted. I told her I was ready to leave. She asked me to wait a few minutes and returned to finish her reefer. Minutes later as we were leaving, to my surprise, the guy who had given me the reefer asked me to return it. I did, and not wanting to appear square, I didn't quiz Julie about what was happening at that apartment or who those people were, but I did tell her I wasn't into reefers.

December came quickly, and the Andy was across the bay in Oakland at the Naval Supply Depot preparing for another run across the Pacific. Jack, a new steward mate, came aboard for duty. He was about thirty, stockily built and boisterous. One morning while in the officer's galley having breakfast, I was pouring corn flakes into a bowl when Jack reached over and attempted to snatch the cereal from my hand for his own use. I pulled the box of corn flakes away from his reach and set it down before me. "Gimme that box," he roared, "or I'll kick your skinny ass." I stood my ground, slowly opening my white serving jacket and revealing the knife under my waist band. And without saying a word, I faced up to Jack and waited for him to make a move toward me. But he backed down, as I had hoped. This incident made the grapevine and reinforced my reputation for standing tall, or as my buddies Bill and Joe put it, "Don't fuck with Slim cause he don't play."

After taking on supplies, the Andy moved back across the bay to San Francisco, to take on passengers for our second run to the Far East. That was when I learned that Dave—the steward mate who had jumped ship—was back aboard the Andy, in the brig. The Shore Patrol had picked him up in the Fillmore District. I felt sorry for him because he was in serious trouble.

Warm thoughts of Julie came to mind on the eve of Andy's departure. We were a good match. She was delighted by my youthful energy and naiveté, and I, fascinated by her savvy and temperament, was satisfied to be her temporary man. Or, in the words of the old blues song, I wanted her to "Let me be your little dog till your big dog come."

Prior to Julie, I was obsessed with the fun and joy of sex. I couldn't get enough, despite visits to the brothel. One night on a street in Fillmore, a sexy lady wiggled up to me and purred, "Do you want to have some fun?" I looked at her and gulped, "Sure." But I wanted more time with her than it took to turn a trick, wanting to spend the entire night realizing my fantasy of nonstop debauchery. So we negotiated a price that I was willing to pay, and off we went to a hotel. Alas, it was then that I learned that there's many a slip twixt cup and lip, for it turned out to be a dumb deal since after the initial romp, each of us fell asleep and slept till dawn.

My relationship with Julie dramatically changed all that, bringing sex on demand with a steadiness that satisfied my raging hormones—early in the morning, in the evening when the sun went down, in the midnight hour, whenever, and without payment in advance.

Early in December, 1946, we steamed out of San Francisco Bay Hoping to get a sign of life, I trained my binoculars on Alcatraz Island, the most irresistible sight in the bay. This was my third time to see it up close, and I had yet to see anybody moving about. It seemed like such a mysterious place, forlorn and desolate. A truly bad scene!

The second run across the Pacific didn't stir up the same level of excitement as the first because we were going to pretty much the same places. The first voyage to the Far East gave me a glimpse of the people there, and I came away with an awareness that they—in their own way—go about their daily lives trying to make a living just like Americans. While I didn't think a second voyage would add much to that, I was ready for a second look.

As before, we left San Francisco for Pearl Harbor and arrived there for the third time. The scenery in the harbor was as familiar as the Hawaiian music, the volcanos and the palm trees. Still, I didn't tire of any of it. My displeasure was in not having any contact with girls like the hula dancers on picture post cards. Bill and I went ashore to Honolulu and met a few girls at a dance hall. But there was nothing native about them, nor were they wearing hula skirts. They were taxi dancers who danced with you on the ballroom floor for the price of a ticket. And it was strictly business. No ticket, no dance.

We were about three days out of Pearl harbor when we crossed the International Date Line, and a strange thing happened. We lost a day in crossing as we had done before, but this time the day we lost was Christmas! When I heard that, I was down-hearted until learning that we would celebrate Christmas nonetheless.

In January, 1947, we anchored off Samar Island in Leyte Gulf, in the Philippines. When I found out where we were, I realized it was the same body of water where my first ship, *Kadashan Bay*, had distinguished herself in what the guys in her skeleton crew called "the greatest naval battle in history," The battle that led to the decline of Japanese naval power and the recapturing of Manila. Looking out at the calm waters, I was awestruck.

That was also a torrid place, causing crew members, including me, to complain about severe heat rash. In hope of relief, with permission from the skipper, some guys jumped from the ship into the water.

As we sailed into Shanghai, a more bustling city than Tsingtao, I thought about the Charlie Chan movies set in Shanghai that I'd seen at the Comet Theater in St. Louis. I also remembered hearing the word "Shanghai" used in movies about sailors and ships—as in he was "shanghaied" or forced to join a ship's crew.

In the harbor, there were cargo ships, barges, junks and sampans, among other vessels. The junks and sampans really held my interest because they looked so simple and easy to build. One morning while looking at them, I wondered if they were durable and guessed it didn't matter, for they were made of easy to get wood and bamboo. Some of the crafts were like houseboats, with people living aboard them. There were also boats, among the lot, that I saw not only in the harbor but also along the coastal waters of China.

Liberty in Shanghai, like Tsingtao, was interesting and fun, and a rickshaw was the best way to get around. I was struck by the politeness and courtesy of the Chinese. Whether merchants or people on the streets, they were very respectful of Americans.

A couple of days after we left Shanghai and were headed for Guam—with a brief stop off Iwo Jima—a mine was spotted bobbing up and down on the Pacific off our starboard side. The Bosun piped General Quarters over the loudspeaker, causing every crew member to rush to his battle station. In addition to their regular duties, steward mates had battle station duties which included serving on gun crews. My battle station was at one of our 5-inch 38 caliber guns. There, I was assigned the task of kicking aside the spent shells. One of our 20 milimeter guns was chosen to explode the mine, and after repeatedly striking it, nothing happened. Somebody said it wasn't a "live" one. Minutes later, General Quarters was canceled. Standing there in my life jacket with the other members of my gun crew gave me a feeling of togetherness.

As the Andy stood off Iwo Jima, I was reminded of the famous picture of marines raising the American flag on Mount Suribachi. It had been less than two years since the marines captured that island, after one of the bloodiest battles in the Pacific. From the Andy, I stared at the island and became caught up in an awesome feeling similar to that I'd felt in Leyte Gulf. As soon as the long boats from the Andy finished carrying passengers to and from the island, we moved on to Guam.

11

Disenchantment

After a brief stop in Guam, we put out for the long crossing to Pearl Harbor and San Francisco. I didn't go ashore as much on the second run across the Pacific as I did on the maiden voyage. Instead, I spent more time aboard ship playing poker—a game in which I had more know how than luck. We played on a bunk taken from its moorings and placed on buckets. And for seats, we sat on buckets which we scrounged.

One afternoon after lunch, a couple of Seabees were still sitting in the almost empty dining room complaining about being bored. One of them called me over to their table and asked, "Where's the action on this tub, the crap games and poker games?" When I told him about our little poker games in the steward mates' compartment, he asked if he and his buddies could join us. "Sure, just let me know when you're ready," I said. "How about tonight?" he asked. I told him to meet me on deck at eight, and I'd take him to the game. With a big smile on his face, he said, "Okay, we'll be there." Knowing they had deep pockets, Bill grinned from ear to ear as I told him about them. "We'll set up a place tonight, and then you can go get 'em," he said.

Bill and I carved out a place in a corner of the head for our Seabees guests. On that first night, three Seabees came to play. A steward mate and I sat in the game to make it five players. Bill ran the game. He was the House Man, dealing five card stud or draw poker. All the players agreed that the cards would "read themselves," meaning a player didn't have to say what cards he held but simply put them face up on the bunk. Ten percent of each pot would go to the House Man. Each evening when there were enough Seabees wanting to play, Bill or I would run a game.

We played with cash, setting minimum table stakes and limits on bets. A typical "big pot" would be about $100.00. Bill and I rotated as House Man, with him running the game one night and me sitting in and vice versa the next night. He kept his cuts from his game, and I kept mine. It was a sweet set up.

One night, however, when I sat in as a player, I had an awful losing streak and lost everything. I took it hard, dropped out of the game and went to my bunk to sulk. I lay there thinking about waylaying the hot-handed Seabee who won most of my money. I could come up behind him and hit him on the head with the butt of my gun, as he returned to his berth, and rob him in the dark passageway. But then I thought, suppose he didn't leave the game alone but was accompanied by another Seabee or two. It would be a sure thing if he left alone. Otherwise, it wouldn't work. I kept brooding over it until I fell asleep.

My experience at losing all my money made me aware of how badly it affected me, and so I changed the way I played. From then on, I set a limit on how much I could stand to lose. And when that limit was reached, I'd drop out and forget it. It was also about that time when I started to focus on how much money could be made by merely being the House Man. And, I soon began to have more fun running the game than playing. When the long voyage was over, I'd earned about $800.00, most of which was sent to my account at First National Bank in St. Louis. Running a poker game on the Andy in the middle of the Pacific Ocean was one of the most thrilling events in my navy career.

In February, 1947, we sailed into San Francisco Bay. Flush with money, I was eagerly looking forward to liberty, and when it was granted, Bill and I headed for our favorite brothel in Fillmore.

My brother James was stationed at an Army base north of Oakland, and we had planned to get together when the Andy returned to the Bay Area. One afternoon, after the ship had moved across the bay to Oakland, I called him and arranged a meeting aboard the Andy. Though we kept in touch, we hadn't seen each other since Christmas of 1945. As he climbed the gangplank to board the Andy, he had to be thinking: "What a difference a year makes."

I asked him what he thought of the ship. He dryly replied, "It's alright." I didn't say it, but I thought to myself, "Come on now. Nobody could fail to be impressed by this humongous ship." But because the Andy was my ship and I was his "little brother," the ship by association with me had to be unimpressive. It was disappointing to see that he hadn't changed. Even when I took him to my locker and showed him some of the money I'd earned at poker, he continued to act out his ho hum thing. It would have been nice if he said something complimentary, but it was okay, for I was overjoyed to be with him again.

We left the ship and took a train to San Francisco. I treated him to dinner and, afterwards, took him to meet the girls at the best little whorehouse in the Fillmore District. "Take your choice and it's on me," I told him. She turned out to be one of my favorites and whispered in my ear that she'd take care of him.

Her curvacious body and flowing black tresses had brother James all shook up, as she led him away. And slightly more than an hour later, after waiting for him at the bar, he returned grinning like the Cheshire cat.

It was March when I caught up with Julie at her hotel, and she invited me to stay over the weekend. I had a 48-hour pass and accepted the invitation. Feeling at home there, I could pause and think about things on my mind. The repeated trips to the Far East and the sense of injustice aboard the Andy had become burdensome. By the time the weekend ended, I'd made up my mind not to make the third voyage but to jump ship.

Early one morning before duty, I was topsides scheming my departure from the Andy. It was still fresh in my mind that Dave was picked up in San Francisco by the Shore Patrol, returned to the ship and put in the brig. The thought of being returned to the Andy was chilling. So I planned to make that unlikely to happen to me, by taking off a day or two before the ship sailed and then leaving the Bay Area for Los Angeles.

I shared my plan with Bill and Joe, hoping they might join me. "We can go down to L.A. and hang out there, until we're ready to turn ourselves in," I said. "Man forget it. I don't want to be locked up in the brig," said Joe. While he wasn't up to facing the music, I thought Bill would come around. He felt as I did about the Andy and was a bit more daring than Joe. It took only a few hours for him to let me know he was coming with me, saying he liked the idea of going down to L.A.

Bill was friendly with the ship's yeoman and found out that the Andy was sailing on March 20 and the last liberty was March 18. So On March 17, I began searching through my personal belongings for things I didn't want to leave behind and stuffed them in a small bag to take with me. From the ship's post office, I mailed my radio, photograph album and gun (which I'd accepted for a bad debt from a hapless poker player) to Babe in St. Louis. The next day, with my money belt strapped around my waist, I was ready to leave the Andy.

On March 17, we took liberty, and according to plan, we avoided the Fillmore District, booking overnight in a hotel near Golden Gate Park. Early the next morning, Bill was still in the sack when I came out of the bathroom and started to get dressed. I asked, "What are we going to do today before we split for L.A. tonight?" I knew Bill to be a cool and easy going guy, but when he said, "Let's play golf," I hesitated, thinking, "Wait a minute, we don't want to be too relaxed." But since Bill was a golf nut who played golf and caddied before joining the Navy, I said, "What the hell, let's do it." And within an hour, we checked out, had breakfast and went to the golf course in a park near the Golden Gate Bridge. With clubs rented from the golf pro, we teed off.

That evening we took a bus to Los Angeles. "I have two uncles living in L.A.," I said to Bill, as he looked out the window. "One of them owns a hotel downtown. When we get there, we'll look him up." Bill asked if I'd ever been to Los Angeles. "No," I said, "but I've heard nice things about it."

Early the next morning, we arrived in Los Angeles, happily mindful that the Andy was sailing the next day, and we were not going with her. Though we didn't expect to see many sailors in L.A., we were struck by their absence in and around the bus station. San Francisco and San Diego were the Navy towns in California—not Los Angeles. In L.A., we felt free to go wherever we wanted without fear of the Shore Patrol. Looking around for a place to have breakfast, we settled on a cafeteria nearby. While munching on some bacon, I pulled out the map of Los Angeles I'd picked up before we left the Bay Area and found that my uncle's hotel was within walking distance, on Ceres near 8th. Street.

Taking in the sights along the way, we noticed that the hotel was in a slightly rundown neighborhood with some vacant buildings that were once small factories. Sprinkled among those buildings were single family frame houses occupied mostly by Chicanos, with a handful of colored people, whites and Asians. My uncle's hotel, called Malcolm Hotel, was only three blocks from "Little Tokyo" on Fifth Street. Some Japanese who lived there before World War II were interned during the war.

In spite of the grungy neighborhood of the hotel, we were satisfied to stay there, for it was off the beaten track and seemed safe. Also, being close to downtown L.A. and only a few blocks from Central Avenue—where we could take a bus into the heart of black L.A.—made us like it even more.

As we approached the hotel, Bill asked me what my Uncle Malcolm was like. I said I didn't know and that this would be my first time to meet him. Upon entering the hotel, I spotted a slightly open door with the word "Office" written on it. We walked in, and I introduced myself to the portly, light-skinned and bespectacled man seated behind the desk and said, "Uncle Malcolm, you look just like your picture. I'm George, your sister Madeline's son."

Uncle Malcolm rose from his seat and, grinning broadly, said, "So you're Madeline's youngest boy," and shook my hand. "I haven't seen you since you were a baby. How nice to see you again so grown up."

"It's nice to see you too," I said, smiling. "This is my friend Bill." Uncle Malcolm shook hands with Bill, as I continued, "We're on leave from our base in San

Francisco and thought it would be fun to come down to L.A. to visit for a while. It would be great if you could rent us a room."

Saying he'd give us the biggest and best room available, he was clearly pleased that we wanted to stay in his hotel. Though it served our purpose well, it was not really my idea of a hotel. If not for the sign "Malcolm Hotel" prominently attached to the building, it could pass for a multiple family house. Each of its four stories consisted of a dozen single rooms. And each room had a wash basin and a closet. A toilet and bathtub were located on each floor at the end of the hall. In this Spartan but clean place, there were no cooking or eating facilities. Its clientele were mainly long-term residents, 30-something, uneducated, low skilled, no skilled, black, from Texas and Louisiana trying to get a foothold in the city.

Shortly after Uncle Malcolm called him to tell him I was at the hotel, Uncle Joseph came to see me. He was Mama's youngest brother, 38, and tall with broad shoulders. "Hya doing?" He asked, giving me a strong handshake. "I haven't seen you since I ran to St. Louis. I know you don't know anything about that. You were just a little boy."

"I don't remember seeing you, but Mama told me about you," I said. "This is my friend Bill. We're down here from San Francisco on leave." After shaking hands with Bill, Uncle Joseph said, "I want you both to come to my house and meet my family before you leave."

Uncle Joseph was a Pullman porter running between the West Coast and Chicago. He lived in South Central L.A. near Central Avenue, a street that Bill and I got to know well because of the night clubs there. His house, which he owned, was in a nice neighborhood. I was struck by the fact that he was the only bread winner in a household of five people which included his wife and three children. He was the first black man I ever met whose wife didn't have to work but could stay home and raise the children.

When Uncle Joseph learned that Bill and I spent time in the clubs and bars on Central, he asked why we were staying so far away from them. He caught me off guard with the question, and I had to think quickly about an answer. Not wanting to tell him the real reason, I simply said, "We like being at Uncle Malcolm's hotel."

At first, I thought Uncle Joseph was nosy and prying with his questions, but when he said he wanted to introduce us to close family friends who had a teenage daughter, I figured he was merely interested in helping us enjoy our stay in L.A. When he took us to meet his friends at their home, it was no surprise to me that when we were introduced to their 18 year-old daughter, Debby, she was smitten by Bill's handsome looks and couldn't keep her eyes off him. Even when responding to a question or point brought up by me, she'd look at Bill and not me. When Uncle Joseph announced that he was ready to leave, Debby asked us to come back the next day, a Saturday, and she'd fix us lunch. We thanked her, and I said, "That's great! We'll see you tomorrow."

From the moment we arrived for Saturday lunch, Debby led the conversation, talking about the sights of L.A. and wanting to show them to us, as she put it, "through my eyes and my girlfriend Alice's." Pausing for a split second, she said, "Let me call her and get her to come over." Neither Bill nor I was interested in hanging out with Debby and Alice. We only accepted the lunch invitation to be polite. Before we had a chance to say yea or nay to the idea of meeting Alice, Debby called her and she was on her way.

Alice wasn't as physically attractive as Debby, but she was smart, ambitious and college bound, reminding me of Joan in St. Louis. She wasn't gushy like Debby and asked me about my Navy experiences as though she was genuinely interested in what I had to say. I enjoyed talking about them and really appreciated her questions. Yet, although she was nice to be with and I was glad to have met her, as Bill reminded me before arriving for lunch, we had other fish to fry, on Central Avenue.

Some of the sexiest colored chicks in the world could be found along a strip of Central Avenue where the hip clubs were located. On any given night, Bill and I were either camped out in Jack's Basket Room, Club Alabam or Down Beat, digging the chicks and the music. It was while listening to saxophone players like Dexter Gordon, Sonny Criss and Wardell Gray in these clubs, that I learned to like jazz.

One night while we were grooving with a couple of fine brown frames and digging the music, a fight broke out. I looked at Bill and said, "Let's get the hell out of here!" We left as the sound of police sirens filled the air, hopping a bus for the hotel. "I guess that's it with the clubs," said Bill.

The next day while having breakfast at a cafeteria, we wondered about our next move, having decided against more carousing on Central Avenue. I said to Bill, "How about Debby and Alice? They're not as much fun, but they're nice to be with." As I poured more milk on my oatmeal and tried in vain to smooth out the lumps, I remembered how pleasant it was talking to Alice and thought clean fun with her and Debby would be nice. "So, what do you say, Bill. Got eyes for that?" I asked. Indifferent, he said, "It's alright with me." So we called Debby and asked her to set up a double date.

On our first date, the four of us went to a movie theater called Florence Mills, in Debby's neighborhood. I asked Alice who Florence Mills was and learned that she was colored and an international singing and dancing star who died at a very early age. I liked it that Alice was so knowledgeable and able to tell me stuff like that.

Bill and I were on our best behavior with Debby and Alice. Going to the movies, playing whist and sightseeing became the things to do with them. While bus riding in South Central Los Angeles, I spoke about how well colored folk seemed to be doing. Alice said that although they were living in neat houses with trimmed little lawns, some of them were poor and constantly jobless.

Back at my uncle's hotel, Bill and I staked out some women who were willing and ready to get it on. Bill and I had only to put a nickle in the juke box situated on the first floor in the back, in a corner, in the dark—and they came. Once they did, we'd dance to Billie Holiday's "Crazy He Calls Me," a tune that became our call to debauchery. Bill and I maintained a nice balance between those women who would and Debby and Alice who shouldn't—even if they would.

I was out in front of the hotel one morning when Uncle Malcolm drove up in his car, parked and walked up on the porch where I was sitting. "Good Morning," I said, "I sure like your car." He said it was in good shape, but it was time to get a newer model. I asked him what he'd take for it. Chuckling at what he regarded as a trivial question, he said, "Oh, I don't know. I suppose I could get a few hundred dollars for it. Why do you ask? Want to buy it?" I wasn't serious when I asked the question, but when I realized I had more than enough money to buy it. I suddenly had a feeling of power.

It was about our 8th. day in L.A., and this was the day the girls were going to take us sightseeing outside South Central L.A. As soon as we arrived, they laid out their plans which included getting on and off a bunch of buses. I sneaked a look at Bill, thinking he felt like me—that it was a bit much to do. When the long day ended, and Bill and I were on the bus returning to the hotel, I said to him, "It was nice seeing what we did, but those buses were a drag."

Ever since the realization that I could afford to buy my uncle's car, I'd imagined doing it. All I needed was a good reason to do it. The day after hopping on and off buses, I had 2 good reasons: sightseeing excursions and tiresome bus rides.

Before telling Bill of my idea to buy my uncle's car, I asked him if he knew how to drive. He said he could but didn't have a license, as if it mattered. We both had to laugh when he said that.

Having made up my mind to buy the car, I caught up with my uncle in his office and asked him if he would sell it to me. He looked at me in disbelief and laughed. "I'm serious," I said.

Utterly amused by the thought of me buying his car, he said, "You are? And what'll you use for money? And if you could buy it, what would you do with it? Take it with you?"

I hadn't thought that much about it, knowing only what I wanted to do with it then. Thinking fast, I said, "I will try to sell it before leaving, and if I can't, maybe you can sell it for me." He liked that answer. Then I offered him $250.00 and said my bank in St. Louis would send the check. He was so taken aback that he was almost speechless and simply said okay. I spared him further shock by not telling him I didn't know how to drive.

Uncle Malcolm considered the deal made and was satisfied that the money was forthcoming from the bank. In the meantime, the big, shiny Oldsmobile sitting at the curb in front of the hotel was mine. I took possesion without bothering with the paper work involved.

With Bill at the wheel, we wasted no time trying it out. It took him a while to smoothly shift gears as the car jerked and sputtered down the street, but I was cool and took that to mean he was simply out of practice. However, when he caromed off two cars parked at the curb, I began to worry. "Hey man," I said, "what's going on? You said you knew how to drive." I told him to pull over and stop the car. During this pause, he said he was just nervous, and that he'd be okay in a minute or so. Then he pulled off and tried it again. And sure enough, his skills improved by the minute, and we both relaxed.

One night after dropping off Debby and Alice and returning to the hotel, Bill and I talked about giving up our freedom and facing the music. "But before we do, let's drive down to Tijuana," said Bill. "Great idea!" I said. "We'll make it our parting shot."

Early the next morning, we took off from the hotel. Soon we were outside Los Angeles on Highway 101 South, laughing and carrying on about some funny stuff that happened during our stay in Los Angeles. Bill was kicking it about 80 miles an hour when steam began to spew from the radiator. We then had to pull off the highway because the car had begun to stall. But before we did, a car coming up behind us collided with our rear end and thrust us sharply against a barrier on the precipice overlooking the ocean. Bill was unhurt, but my forehead crashed against the dashboard, causing acute pain and dizziness.

The driver of the car that struck us stopped and got out to help us. Since I didn't feel too bad, and not wanting to attract attention, we exchanged information from our respective registration cards and let it go at that. We did, however, accept her offer to get us some water for the radiator. True to her word, she returned with a container of water and went on her way. There was no disagreement about turning around and heading back to L.A. And we did, driving carefully through puffs of steam from the radiator and stopping to refill the radiator more than once. What a disappointment, having a car unable to take us 130 miles or so down the road!

It was embarrassing to Uncle Malcolm when I told him about our failure to get to Tijuana. He said he couldn't understand it because the car had never caused him trouble, and he kept it in good running condition. After some discussion, we concluded that the car had been okay before being pushed steadily at 80 miles an hour, and it simply wasn't up to the challenge.

On March 31, we had been AOL (Absent Over Leave) for 13 days and had fewer than 24 hours of freedom left, for we had told everybody that our leave was for two weeks. So after kissing the girls goodbye and telling them we'd write, we began saying goodbye to everybody else. Late that afternoon, Bill and I thanked Uncle Malcolm for his hospitality and told him we were taking off early the next morning. He agreed to take charge of the car—which I left parked in front of the hotel—and see if he could salvage any money out of it for me. I thanked him again and said goodbye.

12

On Ice

On the short ride to the Navy Receiving Station in San Pedro, Bill asked me what I thought was in store for us. I smiled and said the fun was worth whatever they throw at us. We'll do brig time and go on from there. "Yeah," he said with nervous laughter.

"They'll lock us up, but they can't shoot us," I said. "The thing for us to do is to get our story straight and stick to it. Remember it and keep it in mind: We drank too much and decided to sleep it off overnight at a hotel. The hotel didn't give us a wake-up call, and we got up too late to make muster. And since we were already AOL, we didn't see any need to rush back. So we took our time. When we did return, our ship had sailed without us. Not knowing what else to do, we took a bus ride down to L.A., staying until we turned ourselves in at San Pedro."

On arrival at the entrance to the Naval Receiving Station, we stood outside the gate watching the marine sentries checking people entering and leaving the base. Even though I accepted the idea of doing time for committing the crime, it was still a scary situation. Bill was trembling with fear. And I would have been as frightened as he, if not for my ace in the hole. Having waited long enough, I said to Bill, "Let's go, and I'll do the talking."

We then walked up to a sentry at the gate, and I said, "We're AOL. Where do we turn ourselves in?" With a smirk on his face, he said, "Right here. You came to the right place." Within minutes two armed guards showed up and took us straight to the brig.

There, they took us to get prison garb and ordered us to shower. Then, by making us stand at the end of the cell block and read aloud selected passages from a brig rule book, the point was dramatically made that we had to walk the line or catch hell. Following the reading of each passage, the guard asked, "Do you understand?" And we answered, "Yes, sir!" After reading all of the passages, we were given the manual of rules and told to read the rest in our cell. Then they opened the cell door and ordered us to go in.

I said, "Not too bad, eh Bill." By this time he'd relaxed quite a bit.

"Yeah," he said, "so far not too bad."

"We'll be okay. All we have to do is sit it out and stick to our story," I said.

We stepped outside our cell, when the door opened, and marched to the mess hall with other inmates. Following the line, we picked up trays and filled them with food that looked exactly like that in general mess. Then we walked over to our assigned table. This was the routine for each meal, and talking was allowed.

As we became accustomed to the general routines, it was not too bad being in the brig. It helped a lot that we were alone together in a 2-man cell. The scariest thing about the brig were the charges that we heard 3 other inmates were facing: assaulting an officer, robbery of the paymaster, and desertion. The only act of violence in the brig, to my knowledge, happened in a fight between an inmate and a guard. Whatever the issue was between them, they met in the head one night and settled it with a fistfight.

After about 4 days in the brig, we were given a hearing. Called into a room, one at a time, we were asked our account of what had happened to cause us to miss our ship. We each gave the same story that we had rehearsed.

A couple of days after the hearing, the word was out that we and some other prisoners were going to be transferred to the "General Court Martial brig" in San Diego. Although it was only a rumor, it scared the pants off me and Bill. The mere idea of going to that brig meant we would likely be given a General Court Martial. A General was the big daddy of all the court martials, and a conviction by that court carried some heavy penalties. On April 8, the rumor was borne out, and the other prisoners turned out to be none other than the 3 guys we'd heard so much about. Because they gave me a Summary Court Martial—which was only one level below the General—for breaking dishes, I was certain they would give us a General Court Martial for being AOL.

While awaiting transportation to San Diego, the five of us were held in a small room. Sitting next to each other, Bill and I chatted in a low voice. Bill said he couldn't get over being put together with those guys. "They are in deep shit," he said.

"Yeah," I said, "and since I can't see the charges against us being anywhere near as serious as theirs, I wonder why they put us together with them."

The guy charged with desertion was sitting next to me. Referring to the guards taking us to San Diego, I said to him, "Man, those guards are armed to their teeth."

"Yeah," he said. "What are you guys in for?"

I told him we had missed our ship and had been AOL, but we turned ourselves in. He said we were both lucky because if we had been picked up, they could charge us with desertion. He said that was what happened to him. Bill was now listening intently as he told us the story about him leaving his ship without permission. He said he'd been shacking up with his girlfriend who hated his life in the Navy. Demanding that he choose between her and the Navy, he chose her. He'd been AWOL for more than a year when their relationship began to sour. One night she called the cops and had him arrested for slapping her around. The cops checked out his background and discovered he was AWOL. According to him he was charged with desertion rather than AWOL because he didn't voluntarily return but was brought back by the police.

We heard a car pull up and saw a marine come into the room. We guessed he was our driver. To my surprise and horror, 2 armed guards began to put handcuffs and shackles on each of us and then link us together with a chain at the waist. My terror was reduced to resentment and anger over being treated in the same manner as the 3 other prisoners. Two guards with side arms and rifles over their shoulders guided us as we toddled to the station wagon parked about 2 yards away. There, the linking chain was removed as each prisoner entered the vehicle and sat down. Soon we were on coastal Highway 101 enroute to San Diego. Bill looked at me with a faint smile, and I knew exactly what he was thinking: "This was the same highway we started out on for Tijuana a little more than a week ago." I felt sad and mistreated. Tears welled up in my eyes.

We made one restroom stop at a service area on the highway. There, we were all ordered out of the vehicle and stood in a line as the guards determined who wanted to use the restroom. One guard accompanied one or two prisoners at a time, while the other guard stayed with the remaining prisoners at the station wagon. We stood thoroughly shackled and menacing looking, as passers-by stared and sneered at us. I tried to imagine what they thought we had done to deserve this humiliating treatment. After about 3 hours, we arrived at the brig in San Diego and the handcuffs and leg irons were removed. Bill and I were separated from the other 3 prisoners and put in a cell together as before. By then we were almost sick with concern about what was going to happen to us.

Bill said he thought the way we were treated in coming to this brig could only mean that we were going to catch hell from then on. And I thought he was right. After all, this wasn't called the General Court Martial brig for nothing. We were uptight, expecting to come in contact with desperate men and hardened criminals in the mess hall, prison yard and elsewhere outside our cell.

Yet, after a few days of chatting with some of the inmates, Bill and I both began to relax and became less fearful of being roughed up by some malevolent guards or thuggish inmates. The guys we chatted with came across as being pretty decent and believable. They suggested that there was no reason to fear either the guards or inmates. As the days passed I talked to other inmates who, unlike the three prisoners we came to the brig with, happened to have been colored. I got the impression that despite the charges against them, some of them were no more criminal types than Bill and I.

I learned that the General Court Martial brig was not at all like the prison I'd imagined it to be. It was, in fact, like a short-term detention center, a place where prisoners came to be tried and sentenced. After the trial and sentencing, the actual prison time was served elsewhere in places like the penitentiary in Portsmouth, New Hampshire. It was also where a guy already serving a sentence came to appeal the sentence or to get a new trial. Some of the men were impressively knowledgeable about the military judicial system and crime and punishment. Our story about why we were in the brig got on the grapevine and caused the "jail house lawyers" to chuckle and wonder why we were in the same brig with them. More than one of them said to Bill and me, "Don't worry about it. You won't get a General." The "librarian" told us that there wasn't a guy in the brig who wouldn't love to trade places with us. The more we heard talk like that, the more we wanted to believe it. But unlike Bill, who began to think they could be right, I maintained my doubt.

Bill and I stopped thinking so much about our fate and got caught up in the drama of some of the guys around us. One day in the mess hall, we saw Jim, the guy charged with desertion. He told us he had a hearing and was given a General Court Martial, and it was what he'd expected. But his concern was how much time would he have to serve.

We also spoke to inmates who came from the penitentiary where they'd been doing years of hard labor or as one of them put it, "breaking big rocks into little ones." I admired a few of them for their show of hope, optimism and patience. For them, the big concerns were "Will my sentence be dismissed or reduced, or will I have to return to the rock?" There were some lively moments as when just before attending his hearing, you'd hear an inmate say, "I'll see you on the block, or I'll see you on the rock."

After more than 2 weeks in the brig, Bill and I were scheduled for a hearing. It had been delayed because they didn't have our service records from the Andy. We wanted to go ahead with whatever was in store, but, at the same time, we were afraid of what that might be. On the day of the hearing, we appeared separately before the hearing officer, just as we had done in San Pedro. We were asked to tell what happened to cause us to miss our ship, and we repeated the story we'd given before.

For 3 or 4 days after the hearing, we waited nervously for the results. No matter how hard we tried not to let it weigh on our minds, it didn't work. We sweated. And then one morning after breakfast, without any forewarning, we were called back before the hearing officer and told we were given a Summary Court Martial. I was so elated over this news that I had trouble trying to show remorse to the officer. And when I stole a glance at Bill, I could tell he was feeling the same way. We were sentenced to 15 days in the brig and 30 days as a Prisoner-At-Large on the base in San Diego. We shared the news with some of the guys, who said that they weren't at all surprised by the outcome. That was not the case with Bill and me. We were amazed, for we had braced ourselves for worse and saw it as a light sentence. As far as Bill and I were concerned, the whole post-San Pedro thing turned out to be a cakewalk.

On May 8, after having served more than 5 weeks of confinement in both San Pedro and San Diego, Bill and I said our goodbyes to the guys and walked out of the brig into a waiting bus and 2 unarmed guards who escorted us to the Prisoner-At-Large barracks. One of our escorts laughingly said, "You guys ought to be glad to trade the brig for the barracks."

Upon arrival at the barracks, our paper work was quickly processed, and we traded in our brig garb for dungarees and shirts. I searched through a hamper pulling out shirts and pants until I settled for a near fit. Huge letters, "P A L," were stenciled on the back of the shirt. For the next thirty days, PAL was our "Scarlet Letter."

Pariahs though we were, it was okay after we became used to the mocking and jeering of some of the non-PAL population on the base, for we had relative freedom of movement about the base. The recreation hall was the first place we went. There, we were able to shoot pool, play ping pong, and make telephone calls. I also wrote letters, pleased to know that they were no longer censored. Privileges that we had once taken for granted were especially important to us now. And the one we liked the most was being able to go to the mess hall by ourselves whenever we wanted.

Bill and I were put on a work detail every day during the week, Monday through Friday. One day, while hanging over the side of a ship, in dry dock, we performed a seaman type job: chipping paint. The tedium involved in that work was brain numbing. I prayed that on the next day, they would give us a task more in keeping with our branch of the Navy, like cleaning and waxing the floors of the officers' lounge. But we had no such luck and spent at least a week removing old rusty paint. Yet, being a PAL wasn't a bad deal on the whole. And we were always comforted by the knowledge that it would end after 30 days.

On June 8, our PAL sentence ended, and we returned to active duty. Since I had fewer than six months of my 2-year enlistment left, and Bill had more than a year to serve, we thought he would be assigned to another ship, and I'd finish my term on the base in San Diego. Well, it was just the reverse. I boarded another another ship and he remained on the base.

Over the past year, Bill and I had become close friends. Our relationship taught me the joys of friendship. His temperament and other qualities made it a genuine pleasure to be around him. He was the coolest cat I ever knew. His parting words, "So long Slim. Let's keep in touch," reflected his easygoing, straight ahead attitude.

On June 12, I joined the crew of a destroyer, the *U.S.S. Shelton (DD790)*. Service on sea-going ships was the primary reason for my enlistment, and even in the waning months, service on another one was just great. Then, I could proudly say at the end of my enlistment that I had served on three warships: an aircraft carrier, a troop ship and a destroyer. The *Shelton* was almost brand new, having been commissioned only a year before I came aboard. Also being a crew member of a warship based in San Diego was not a bad deal, for I had grown to like San Diego even from my limited view from the base. It was good to be back on active duty. And after more than 2 months without liberty, I looked forward to going ashore—legitimately.

13

Bravado

Shortly after boarding the *Shelton*, the news of my court martial and brig time got on the ship's grapevine. Some of the steward mates who heard it saw me as a cool, tough and hip salt, and they looked up to me. I enjoyed the reputation for toughness and began to see myself in that light. Consequently, I adopted a dual attitude, shifting from a nice guy to a combative one, depending upon the situation and audience. You could see it in my walk and hear it in my talk.

One night while on liberty and dressed in civilian clothes, I was standing in front of a bar chatting with a shipmate. Suddenly another steward mate rushed up to us, and looking at me, said a guy down the street was trying to pick a fight with a steward mate from our ship. "Let's go." I said, "Show him to me." When we reached the scene, I saw a guy holding our shipmate's necktie in his hand and heard him say, "I ought to cut this fucking thing off." I walked in front of him with my knife in my hand, grabbed his wrist and asked, "Do you wanna cut my tie off too?" Startled, he quickly released the mate's tie, stepped back from him and me and abruptly took off running down the street. Spurred on by my shipmates, I took off after him, swinging my six inch blade. I had just about caught up with him when he reached the curb, tripped and fell to his knees. Kneeling in the gutter, he pleaded, "Don't cut me!" I said, "Get up you son-a-fa-bitch and apologize to my friend." He stood up and cried out that he was sorry and took off again. I let him go, feeling relieved. I had put on quite a show and lived up to my badass image. And that was enough.

San Diego was a very likeable city. I ranked it second to San Francisco, with Los Angeles coming in third. It was in San Diego that I went to a huge dance hall unlike any other I'd ever seen. The orchestras playing there included black-folk favorites like T Bone Walker and Lionel Hampton. And, the dancers in the hall which was not in a colored neighborhood, included people of all colors and races.

In August, 2 months after boarding the *Shelton*, I learned to my surprise that I was eligible for leave and was granted a 30-day pass. It had been more than a year and a half since I was in St. Louis, and during that time I was not homesick a single day, but I did want to see my family. And I was especially eager to see my brother Ben, who had returned home from the war. So I took a train to St. Louis.

The train ride from San Diego to St. Louis was long but not boring, for the scenery was new and interesting. I had come by sea, on the Andy, to California and had not seen landscape west of the Mississippi River in the Southwest. After three nights and a couple of days, the train pulled into Union Station in St. Louis.

I left the station and took a taxi up to Lawton to see Babe and the Ole Man. After making the first stop in the shared taxi, my turn came and the driver dropped me off in front of the house. It was as forbidding as the hot steamy weather, and its occupants were sitting on the stoop hopelessly in search of comfort. I made my way up the steps, smiling in recognition of familiar faces among them, and on to the apartment. I knocked, and Babe opened the door crying out, "Baby, come on in here! Let me look at you." We stood hugging each other, happy to be together again. "I bet you ain't had a good meal since you left here," she said. "Are you hungry Baby?"

"No, I'm fine," I said, as I stretched out on the sofa and tried to stay awake, while listening to Babe talking up a storm. Sitting for days on the train without much sleep had caused me to nod. But when Babe began to give her account of an F.B.I. agent who came looking for me when I was AOL from the Andy, I stopped nodding and sat up.

She said it was about three o'clock in the morning when she heard a slow and steady tap, tap, tap on the door. She tried to get the Ole Man to go to the door, but he was fast asleep and wouldn't budge. So she went to the door saying to herself, "Who the hell is that knocking on my door at this time of morning?" She called out, "Who's that?" And this is what she said happened:

"A man slowly said F…B…I…Is George there? George is in the Navy, I told him. He said, where is George? I said, you oughta know where my baby is. He's in the Navy! And then opening the door a little, I asked him, what's this all about? He said you were missing. And I said, missing where? What y'all done with my baby? He saw that I didn't know what he was talking about and left his card, saying I should get you to call him if you showed up."

Over the years, Babe would repeat that story at my prompting, and each time she did, I'd crack up.

The Ole Man didn't come home until around midnight, drunk as usual. Babe said the Ole Man knew I was in the Navy and was troubled because he didn't know how it happened. She always succeeded in being vague on the subject whenever he brought it up. Since my enlistment period was coming to an end in a few months, I saw no need to continue avoiding the issue of my being in the Navy, and, given an opportunity, I was ready to talk to him about it.

Mama, like the Ole Man, didn't know the details of my enlistment, but unlike him, she demanded a full accounting from me. In my letters to her, I had declined to go into it, but she still insisted on knowing. As much as I wanted to see Mama, I wasn't going to discuss my enlistment with her. For fear that this was what she expected if I went to visit her, I decided to put off the visit. As far as I was concerned, my enlistment was in the past, and I needed to focus on its end—not its beginning.

When Ben, who didn't know about the tension between Mama and me, came by the Ole Man's to get me to go with him to see Mama, I decided to go. He told me Mama was going through periods of depression, and it would help for her to see me. So I went, but I didn't talk about my enlistment.

One day while sitting around the Ole Man's apartment and bored to tears, I thought of Joan and found her telephone number. Joan and I had stopped writing before I left the Andy, and now that I was back in St. Louis, I wondered how things were going and called her. She was in town for the summer, and said she was glad to hear from me, telling me to come right over. We were happy to see each other again, hugging in a warm embrace. After laying out some snacks and soft drinks, she brought me up-to-date on current and past events. She was a sophomore at Howard University and things were working out as she hoped and planned. I told her I'd met some girls, Debby and Alice, in Los Angeles who reminded me of her in many ways. When I mentioned that I would be out of the Navy in a few months, she asked, "What do you want to do when you get out?" Since I hadn't thought about life beyond the Navy, she caught me unprepared to answer. I thought to myself, "I guess it is time to start thinking about it."

After nearly 3 long weeks in St. Louis, I had enough and returned to California. The *Shelton* was sailing up the California coast to San Francisco, and I had been ordered to meet her there when my leave expired. Meeting my new ship in the same port in which I fled the old one was a little strange.

From Joe's letters, I knew the Andy, still making voyages to the Far East, would not be in port at that time. Too bad, for it would have been fun to see the Andy, Joe and the guys again. And showing off the *Shelton* would have given me much pleasure. Nonetheless, it was great merely to be back in the Bay Area.

Many times when in the Bay Area, I was aware of Treasure Island, a man-made island situated in the bay slightly north of the Oakland Bay Bridge. I was intrigued by its name, supposedly inspired by Robert Louis Stevenson. It was linked by a causeway to another famous island, Yerba Buena, known by sailors as YBI. I never imagined ever seeing either of these islands up close. But, once again the unexpected happened, and there I was at the Naval Station on Treasure Island, awaiting the arrival of the *Shelton*.

While waiting, I didn't waste any time in going to the Fillmore District to look for Julie. To my surprise, she was neither at the bar nor the hotel. I wondered what happened to her and was surprised by how badly I wanted to see her again. Fillmore, though, like my favorite house of pleasure where I returned to renew old acquaintances, was still jumping with joy.

In early September, the *Shelton* sailed into the bay. My pleasure in seeing her again was lessened by the news that she was putting back out to sea for San Diego without much delay. Duty aboard her was sweet and morale was high. Her only shortcoming was her lack of voyages overseas. Her mission, at the time, was to maintain readiness by way of exercises and maneuvers off the coast of San Diego.

Tijuana, Mexico was nearly 20 miles from San Diego, and I was determined to go there at least once. One night opportunity knocked while carousing in San Diego with two buddies from the ship. The bars closed before we were ready to call it quits, and somebody shouted, "Let's go to Tijuana. The bars are still open there!" And with me in total agreement, we took off. There, after a round of drinks which included Tequila for me, we left the bar, got in a taxi and told the driver to take us to the girls. He took us to some hovels alongside a huge smelly ditch on the outskirts of town. He parked and briefly left the taxi to talk to a man who'd just stepped out of one of the shacks. Upon his return to the taxi, he told us we'd have to wait. Meanwhile, my head and stomach were playing a game of chicken. (Which would be the first to give in to the raging mix of beer, whiskey and Tequila?) I wanted to take a rain check on the whole thing and return to the *Shelton*. But the man from the shack suddenly reappeared and beckoned to us to come in. We did and found three young curvaceous women waiting for us. My two buddies and I settled on our choices and were led to separate places.

My choice guided me to a squalid shack, steps away from the main one. As she undressed, a hot summer breeze wafted across her body, making its lack of hygiene apparent and offensive. I then snapped at her in a loud angry voice, "You stink! No sex with a dirty bitch!" Pushing her aside, I yanked my pants back up, stumbled out of the shack and fell into the taxi.

While slouching in the back seat, waiting for the guys and the driver to return, a young slightly built fellow appeared about three feet away and began to pace back and forth along the length of the taxi. He glowered and pointed a finger at me, muttering something incomprehensible. I was unable to get a clear reading of the situation, in my mental state, but he was definitely bothered by something and had bad intentions toward me. His menacing gestures held my attention, causing me to think there was a connection between him and the bad smelling woman whom I rejected.

I slowly sat up straight, taking out my knife and opening it while keeping a keen eye on him. He stooped to pick up a tree branch and came close to the taxi angrily mumbling something. I didn't believe he dared mess with a sailor in the U.S. Navy. But he did. Approaching the taxi with the branch in his hands, he thrust it through the open window at my face, without success. Then, in order to better control the movement of the long branch, he placed it on the window frame and poked it at my face with one hand while gripping the window frame with the other. I then swung my knife at his hand on the frame, causing him to quickly withdraw it, step back, and pull his branch with him.

As he stood there trying to figure out his next move, it dawned on me that he must be either her pimp, her husband, her brother or somebody angry with me for the way that I treated the unclean young woman. Suddenly, upon hearing my buddies returning to the taxi, my antagonist dropped his branch and disappeared into the darkness. Seconds later, the driver returned and drove us back to town. So much for Tijuana and its suburbs.

One day while serving officers in the wardroom, a steward said to me, "Go to the yeoman's office as soon as you can." I asked what it was about, and he said he didn't know. What could the yeoman want to see me about, I wondered. When I went to see him, he shocked me with orders to leave the ship on September 30—one week away—for the separation center on the base. My two-year enlistment in the Navy was coming to an end several weeks earlier than I anticipated. In the waning days aboard the *Shelton,* I found myself thinking a lot about the good times I enjoyed while serving aboard both the *Shelton* and the Andy.

Commissioned fewer than two years, the *Shelton* and her crew were new and represented the future. Feeling like a member of the entire crew, I was always happy to be aboard. The Andy, on the other hand, represented the past. Her leadership appeared unable to shift easily from a war-time mission of transporting combat troops to a peace-time one of transporting women passengers. She was an old dog in the throes of learning new tricks. Although I liked her for the wonderful voyages and experiences she made possible, I hardly saw myself as a member of the whole crew but as a steward mate—separate and unequal.

On September 30, 1947, I left the *Shelton* for the separation center and the beginning of a process that led to an honorable discharge. I entered the separation barracks with bittersweet memories of the past two years, but, with all things considered, there was much more pleasure than pain. Yet, when asked, during the separation process, if I wanted to re-enlist or join the Navy Reserve, I answered no—knowing that I had enough.

Like me, some departing steward mates didn't have great expectations about what they were going to do as civilians. A typical question making the rounds among these guys was "What are you gonna to do when you get out?" And the common answer was "I don't know." The seamen I chatted with weren't unsure about what they were going to do. One guy who'd been a pipefitter was looking forward to becoming a plumber and was smuggling his tools out with him. Others talked about opening businesses relating to some skills they'd picked up in the Navy. The white guys were clearly expecting to do big things and were eager to get out and pursue their goals.

Not knowing what I was going to do wasn't the only part of my vague future, for I didn't even know where I was going to live. As much as I liked San Francisco, having seen it primarily from the perspective of a sailor on the prowl for fun and sex, the thought of living there as a civilian never crossed my mind. Los Angeles, on the other hand, was a different story because I saw it through the eyes of Alice, Debby and my relatives, and I liked it enough to consider living there.

But, even though living in St. Louis was out of the question, wanting to work on building a good relationship with Mama and to hang out with my brothers, I decided to go there.

14

Meandering

On October 6, 1947, as a 16-year-old veteran, I returned to St. Louis. Taking a taxi from Union Station, I went straight to the Ole Man's place. To my amazement and disappointment, he and Babe were no longer living there. And neither old nor new tenants could tell me anything about their whereabouts. It was the strangest thing, for when I was there with them only two months earlier, there wasn't a hint of their intention to move. I was completely mystified.

I left there and went to see Mama. She answered the door with a look of surprise, saying she hadn't expected me to come back so soon. Smiling, she said, "Come on in and tell me what happened." I explained that I was discharged several weeks early. She said I couldn't have come at a better time, for Ben had moved out, and I could take his room. I thought to myself, "Mama sure is in a good mood. I hope it lasts." She'd assumed that I wanted to stay with her, and though I had considered renting a furnished room nearby, I went along with her. Maybe by living with her, that loving feeling we had for each other might break lose and express itself better—I hoped.

I sure wished Mama was more like Babe in showing her love for me. Babe, unlike Mama, expressed it freely, openly and wherever. For example, there was the time I had diptheria. Babe came home from work and found me sick with a high fever. Right away she got Ben to help rush me to the hospital. There, in the emergency room, after waiting longer for medical attention than she thought I should, Babe yelled, angrily to the nurses as well as anybody wearing a white smock, "Somebody better see about my baby right now. He's got a high fever and he's been waiting too long!" And, yes, I felt a wee bit embarrassed, but more importantly, I felt cared about and loved.

"I don't know how long I can do it, but I am going to try and live in harmony with Mama," I told myself. It was annoying that Mama still saw me as her little boy, even though I had just returned from a two-year hitch in the Navy. Seeing myself as a man, maybe not full grown but a man nevertheless, I expected to be treated as such by Mama and everybody else. But I was ready to cut her some slack because of who she was.

"Come on Mama let's go to the show," I'd say to her at times. And off we'd go on the streetcar down Finney Avenue to the Comet Theater. And I sometimes took her to the candy shop where the clerk asked if we were sister and brother. Mama really liked that. Sadly, I can't recall Mama ever taking the lead and saying she'd like to go out and do one thing or another—just to have some fun. In fact, I don't know of an occasion for her to say that to anybody. Regrettably, fun eluded her much of her life.

As soon as I could, I reported to the Veterans Administration to find out how I could get my "52-20;" that is, 20 dollars per week for 52 weeks. That was a GI Bill benefit available to veterans while looking for a job—a kind of unemployment insurance. When I showed up to apply for the benefit, I was fearful of opening Pandora's box and exposing Mama's unbelievable child-bearing history. According to military service records, she was the mother of two sons born four months apart, one in July and another in November. Luckily, that fact didn't jump out of the box.

Despite Mama wanting to boss me around, I enjoyed being back around family. Ben, whom I looked up to and chatted with a lot, was not only my oldest brother but my best friend. Still, in general, life in St. Louis was humdrum.

One afternoon as I stood waiting for my cousin, Harold, to respond to his doorbell, I noticed a tall, svelte young lady entering a house down the block. I loudly called out to him, "Quick, open up. There's somebody I want you to see." But he was too slow. She had gone into the house, before he saw her.

"Who were you talking about?" he asked. When I described her, he said, "That sounds like Mary. She lives there."

"What do you know about her? I sure would like to meet her," I said.

He called his wife Marsha into the living room and told her I wanted to meet Mary. Marsha knew her well and told me that she had walked the straight and narrow throughout Sumner High School: no hanging out with girls or boys but into books, piano lessons and church. And she was about to graduate from college and start a teaching career.

I told myself, "Hey, this is my kind of girl." Not only was she eye-catching but educated and talented. At my urging, Marsha called Mary and arranged for her to drop by the next day to meet me. Upon meeting and seeing her up close, I liked her even more. Her pretty face, flowing dark hair, extending below her narrow feminine shoulders, and mocha-colored skin were a joy to gaze upon.

On our first date, we went to a "Jazz at the Philharmonic" concert at Kiel Auditorium, a truly memorable event. With each of us 6 feet in height, we were a striking couple, drawing the attention of other concert goers. Having her clinging to me as we maneuvered through the crowd in the auditorium and being attentive to my slightest utterance was thrilling. The program featured outstanding jazz soloists, including the pianist, Oscar Peterson who, dressed in formal attire and wearing argyle socks in plain view, performed brilliantly and earned much praise from Mary.

Mary had broad interests. And whenever she asked me to talk about places I'd been, I was delighted. A regular refrain was "Tell me what the people are like" in such and such a place. She was fascinated by my stories, especially the ones carefully selected about San Francisco and Shanghai.

She didn't know I'd never completed a single high school course. So when she urged me to return to school, she had no idea that I'd have to start as a freshman. Nor did she know that I was a 14-year-old boy when I joined the Navy. She was almost 22 and thought I was about her age. Speaking like a real teacher, she'd say, "You're never too old to go to school." This lovely lady was my ideal woman, but her world of education and culture was much too advanced. And I wasn't ready to try and work my way into it by starting with high school in St. Louis, even under her gentle persuasion. So it wasn't long before we drifted apart.

Cousin Harold's world, on the other hand, was perfect for me. It was my great escape from the tedium of daily life in St. Louis. I thought it was cool that he didn't have a regular 9-to-5 but was a juke box maintenance man with irregular hours. I'd hang out with him as he made his rounds in black and white joints in the county. Records on the juke box that got a lot of play were kept on the box—no matter how old they were. And records that didn't get a lot of action were replaced. Harold kept notes on which records people played repeatedly in all the joints, and with some advice from the bartenders he'd decide on what to do. He kept the juke boxes well oiled and humming and the joints jumping. One afternoon, a fine white chick slinked over to the juke box and purred, "Put something good on there." Smiling at her, Harold said, "They're all good," and played a funky record that caused her to snap her fingers and shake her booty. It was like that in more than one red-neck joint—and always fun to watch the mutually tantalizing performances.

Harold and I were kindred spirits. Like me, he was determined to do his thing and resisted anything that interfered with him doing so. We clicked without trying, and though he was seven years older than I, he treated me as an equal. Whenever he thought he could turn me on to something of interest, he'd do it.

One night while sitting around in his living room, he talked about Henry Wallace who was then campaigning for president. He asked me to come with him to Wallace's local campaign office to see what it's like. He was covering the 1948 campaign of the local branch of the Progressive Party, for a black newspaper, and would get me a press card.

I jumped at this opportunity and went with him. At the campaign office I was struck by the collegial spirit of the white and colored people working there. A few of them said that as president, Wallace would improve the lot of black folk all over the country. That was exciting stuff to hear. And it wasn't hard to believe, as I watched his campaign workers of different skin colors caught up in a flurry of activity and united in their cause. Everybody was so warm and friendly that I wanted to take part in what they were doing.

Meanwhile back at Mama's, she was still complaining about the late hours I was keeping and telling me to find a job. "Get up early," she'd say, "and get out in the streets and look. You won't find anything staying in the bed." My mustering out pay and 52-20 were tiding me over nicely, and I felt no need to get a regular job. Yet I wanted her to stop nagging me, for fear that the tension between us might increase. As much as I wanted to continue my free and easy lifestyle, I decided to stop staying out late and find a job.

One morning I went downtown to talk to a buddy about a job shining shoes. He operated a three-chair-shoe-shine stand in a shop that blocked felt hats. I took one of the chairs on a part-time basis; with tips it paid well. It was fun working with my friend, Reed. He didn't talk much, but when he did, it was thoughtful and often funny. He could tell by sight if a customer was likely to stiff you or give you a tip. Under his guidance I became expert at shining shoes, working three or four days a week.

Yet, throughout the three months I held that job, Mama kept saying, "Find a full-time job." Once again trying to keep the peace between us, I found a 9-to-5, as a kitchen helper at a Washington University fraternity house. The house mother was impressed with my work experiences in the Navy and hired me. The whole concept of fraternity and house mother was totally new and intriguing to me. I was struck by the support services available to the young guys in that all-white fraternity. Their food was of the best quality and readily available. I said to myself, "With this kind of support, how could a guy fail to do well in college. This is a great life!" I paid attention to the fraternity members, observing them and listening to what they said to each other. But they were always on the move, often rushing into the dining room or through the kitchen, allowing little opportunity for me to chat with them as I wanted.

After a few months on that job, I was ready to move on. But before I left, a retired principal of a black school, Mr. Washington, who waited tables in the fraternity house on special occasions, passed on some advice that I considered. He had heard me cussing like a sailor. I'd say things like "What the fuck is this?" and "I don't give a shit." Late one afternoon, he called me aside and with one hand on my shoulder and looking me straight in the eyes, quietly said, "Why do you use such foul language? You can express yourself without using bad words." Long after I had left that job, I thought about what he said and how he said it—as I tried to cool it with the profanities.

By December, 1948, I had failed to build the close relationship with Mama that I wanted. No matter how I tried, it just didn't happen. I guessed it wasn't meant to be, since she wanted to control me, and I had to be free and independent. My brothers were busy working and raising their children. And Babe and the Ole Man had vanished without a trace. So, being with family was no longer a reason to be in St. Louis, and I decided to take off.

15

Another Look

In the last week of December, I boarded a train for Los Angeles, my fourth train trip between Missouri and California. The novelty was long gone, and it was merely a long boring ride with little to do while passing through familiar scenery. As I sat looking out the window, feeling excited about my return, the great times Bill and I had in Los Angeles while AOL came to mind. It had been almost 2 years since then.

On January 1, 1949, the train arrived in Los Angeles, and I was greeted by the warmth and sunshine of the city. I left the station and went straight to Uncle Malcolm's hotel. He'd received my letter saying I was coming and was glad I planned to stay at his hotel. I immediately asked about the car. He said it had sat on a lot in disrepair for more than a year, and he gave it to the lot owner in exchange for what was owed in rental charges. "I'm sorry it turned out that way," he said, "but I didn't have time to do anything else with it." I thought that if I had written to him about it, maybe things would have turned out differently. Too bad, for I could really use it now.

James, whom I hadn't seen since I took him to that groovy whorehouse in San Francisco almost 2 years ago, was now living in Los Angeles at Uncle Joseph's house. After his discharge from the Army, he remained in California without returning to St. Louis even to visit. St. Louis had no lure for him. Mama was the only person there with whom he had contact, and that was sparse. When he came to see me at the hotel, I noticed he'd grown taller and was now about 6 feet, 2 inches and weighed about 170 pounds. His ruddy complexion was prominent under the California sun.

Smiling broadly and more formal than ever, James said, "Welcome to Los Angeles. Glad to see you back in California." When it came to showing that he was glad to see you, he had his own peculiar way of doing that—a wide smile. I was more demonstrative than he and gave him a firm handshake and a hug.

Since his discharge in California and subsequent move to Los Angeles, he had been living a Spartan and disciplined life. His only source of income was the small stipend he received as a student under the GI Bill. He was studying music: voice and trumpet, while renting a room in Uncle Joseph's home. Uncle Joseph didn't see any connection between James's musical ambitions and making a living and therefore concluded he was wasting his time and should try and find a job. Being the outspoken person he was, Uncle Joseph shared this opinion not only with him but with others as well, to James's dismay. When I said to James, "Let's share a large room in Uncle Malcolm's hotel, instead of paying rent in two different places," he liked the idea and wasted no time in moving in with me.

While James did his thing, I did mine, spending lots of time strolling over to nearby downtown L.A. and taking in the sights, outdoors and indoors. Burlesque shows became my favorite indoor treat. I never tired of gaping at the voluptuous strip-tease dancers and laughing at the funny routines of the comedians.

About 100 yards from the hotel was a parking lot on 8th. Street that caught my interest. It was a remnant of better days when the area enjoyed much more industrial and commercial activity. There was something noteworthy on the property: a small building under lock and key with three chairs for seating customers having their shoes shined. Often I'd peered through the window and noticed that the interior was in very good condition, needing only some soap, water and elbow grease to put it in working condition. Uncle Malcolm told me it belonged to the owner of the cafeteria down the block.

One afternoon I went to talk to him, introducing myself as the nephew of the owner of Malcolm Hotel. I asked him to let me spruce up the lot and attend the cars of his breakfast and lunchtime trade. He agreed to let me do it. And in exchange for my car parking services, I got a free breakfast and the right to all the profits from shining shoes. I was elated over what I'd imagined to be good prospects for making some money. Well, it turned out that the car owners were more interested in what the cafeteria was dishing out than getting their shoes shined. The tips from parking cars were as few as the shoes to shine. But that was okay, for I was at least assured of a great breakfast five days a week.

Uncle Malcolm, in addition to managing the hotel he owned, managed another hotel, the Silver City, a block away on Kohler Street. They were basically alike in every way, including their patrons. There at Silver City, I was quickly befriended and soon became privy to the Saturday night poker games held weekly by some residents. Having no money, I merely stood around watching the game. One night, there was an old guy sitting in the game who had a habit of fiddling with his cards after he dropped out. I didn't mention it to anybody, but I believed he was marking cards.

He was quiet, unassuming and easily overlooked, with the manner of a gentleman, dressed in a suit, shirt and tie. I was intrigued by him. One night before the game started, I spoke to him and told him of my love for poker and how I'd run games on the high seas in the Navy. He found that interesting, and we became chummy, with him telling me about his travels from city to city playing poker and the horses. Until then, I had never heard of anybody making a living that way and found it fascinating.

Before he moved on to another town, he let me in on a trick of the trade. "You only need to mark one or two aces, kings and queens to get an edge," he said. "Just scratch the back of 'em." Demonstrating with a small piece of sandpaper stuck on the inside of his finger—next to his pinky—he placed a card between the sandpaper finger and his thumb and abraded its corner. The abrasion on the card was so slight that unless you knew what to look for, you wouldn't know it was there. "Hey," I excitedly said to him, "that's something!" Though much impressed, I figured it would take somebody with his avuncular appearance and manner to pull it off without raising suspicion.

I thought that old gambler had a great life: living by his wits, free and easy on the road and unbeholden to anybody. He inspired me to want to be a professional gambler. My first idea in that direction was to book races at Santa Anita with residents of the two hotels, for starters. But then after thinking it through, I could see that the idea was loaded with too many complications and problems, and I forgot it. Running poker games was a much better idea, and something I knew how to do. So I pursued it.

When laying out my poker game plan and need of a room to Uncle Malcolm, he listened, but thought it wouldn't work. "I can't even depend on a lot of 'em to pay rent on time," he said, "so I don't see how they can have money for poker." Yet, knowing I'd once made money running poker games in the Navy, he gave his approval with the proviso that the games were run so as not to disturb others or to attract undue attention.

In the basement of the hotel, I found a table and some chairs and put them in the small third floor room which I dubbed the "Poker Room." I was proud of my setup. The games began with guys from the hotel, playing for nickles and dimes, and so I didn't cut the pots. As word got out about the Poker Room, I began getting some of the overflow from the Silver City game. One night, for the first time, the pots were big enough to cut.

Annie, a street walker who lived with her pimp, Jim, on the second floor, was a tall, shapely redhead from Texas. Occasionally she'd sauntered into the Poker Room just to kibitz and kid around with the guys. Thinking it might be good for business, I encouraged her to come. But a night that promised to be a bonanza turned into a disaster. Two guys from Silver City with serious money came to play. One of them asked if Annie was going to show up. I said, "I'll see to it that she does," and sent my helper to get her. Minutes later, she sashayed into the room smiling and came over to me. "To you guys who don't know her, this is Annie," I said. The guy who'd asked about her took her hand and pulled her over to him. She went into her seductive act, as she stood glued to him, running her fingers through his hair and resting her hand on his shoulder.

She had been in the room for about 5 minutes when Jim was heard coming down the hall yelling, "Annie!" I thought it odd for him to be calling her aloud in the hall, but I didn't dwell on it. Suddenly, he rushed into the room and without warning lunged at Annie, pulled her back from the player, punched her to the floor and dragged her out of the room as she screamed and begged him to stop. Meanwhile the players, fearful that the loud commotion was going to bring the cops, stuffed their pockets with money from the table and raced out of the door.

Within 5 minutes all the players had left the hotel, and the Poker Room was closed and locked. I felt awful about what had happened to Annie and went to see about her. To my surprise it was she who answered the door. Holding a wet towel to her pummeled face, she let me come in. Then turning away, she went to the edge of the bed where Jim sat crying hysterically. In her sobbing voice, Annie said to him, "It's alright baby. I know you didn't mean it." I asked her, "Don't you want to go to the hospital?" She brushed off the idea as though it was totally out of the question. That whole thing was completely puzzling to me. She had been brutally knocked about only minutes ago, and now here she was nursing her wounds and refusing to go to the hospital, while at the same time trying to comfort her brutal and doped-crazed pimp.

The next morning when Uncle Malcolm arrived, he heard about the commotion and sent for me to explain what happened. As he listened to me, I could tell by his facial expression that my poker game enterprise in the hotel was over.

Helping in the operation of both hotels, seeing to it that the laundry and maid services were efficient and reliable, was Uncle Malcolm's wife, Aunt Lillian. In a gentle and insinuating manner, she often let me know that she didn't think much of my behavior, especially the part involving the loose women in the hotel. She had high expectations of me, urging me to think about going to college. More than once, she said to me, "If you go to college and finish, I'll buy you a convertible." I thought that was a wonderful thing to say. But attending college was about as likely as getting rich shining shoes at the parking lot.

She and Aunt Dorothy, Uncle's Joseph's wife, were refined women who were born in Los Angeles and graduated from high school there. Aunt Dorothy, like Aunt Lillian, tried to motivate me and get me on the straight and narrow. She was especially fond of the fine arts and tried to interest James and me in them by taking us to the art museum in Exposition Park.

James was committed to the performing arts—singing and the trumpet. When he told me of his plan to sing in an amateur program at Clifton's Cafeteria in downtown Los Angeles, thinking it was a cool idea, I questioned him about it and learned that at the very least each performer was given a consolation prize. He said he was going to prepare for the event by going to the library to borrow music to the song he intended to sing, namely, "You'll Never Walk Alone." I asked him to get me a copy of "Trees," because I planned to sing too.

As it happened, we were the last two singers to sign up for the program, and this meant we were the first to sing. I preceded James and was introduced by my first and middle name because James urged me not to use our last name which he chose to use. He laughingly explained, "If they think we're related, your bad singing will make me look bad too." He said he was serious about winning.

Clifton's was beautifully decorated with artistic water works, and the dinner crowd was a middle class audience who ate and chatted as the singers performed for them on the huge stage. After each performance, the diners applauded and an applause meter recorded it. A singer would have to reach a certain point on the meter to become a finalist. Each finalist was then asked to stand by, until all the singers had sung, and be judged against all the finalists. Each singer failing to become a finalist was immediately given a certificate of appreciation and led off the stage. The certificate was a consolation prize good for as much food as a tray could hold.

As I'd anticipated, I was given the certificate immediately after finishing my song. Then I left the stage to listen to James from the wings. When he finished, and I heard the weak applause, I motioned to him to come and join me at the food counter. He ignored the gesture, giving me a look of disapproval, and remained in the wings. I proceeded to the food area, expecting to be joined by him before loading up my tray. When James—looking dejected and complaining it was unfair that he wasn't one of the finalists—caught up with me, I had just begun to pick up my silverware.

I lived a foot-loose and fancy-free existence which kept me on the edge of survival and often in need of more than my parking lot earnings. So sometimes I'd take off, join James, at dawn, and head for the farm workers' gathering place, to hitch a ride to the farmlands of San Joaquin Valley. In the valley near Bakersfield, we picked cotton til dusk. It was hard but sweet because we got paid on the spot. The more we picked the more we earned. I always left there with enough money to tide me over for a while.

By May, 1949, after 4 months in L. A., I had begun to tire of my care-free lifestyle and living on the margin of existence. One Saturday morning while having breakfast in a restaurant in Little Tokyo with James, who kept up with Veterans Administration happenings, he mentioned some openings for "food service workers" at a V.A. hospital. Having no interest in a regular job himself, James merely spoke of it as a matter of information. It got my attention and I thought, "Maybe I should look into it." I did and got the job.

The hospital was way out on Sawtelle Avenue near Santa Monica, more than an hour's bus ride which was almost entirely on Wilshire Boulevard. Man, what a world of beauty! That was the impression I got while peering through the window of the bus at the grand mansions amid striking gardens and huge areas of manicured lawns along the way. Alluring and expensive looking shops lined the boulevard, adding to the beautiful and well-ordered visual treat. It was virtually an all-white world, for I never spotted a colored person the full length of the bus ride, except for some women who appeared to be domestics.

The hospital was located in West Los Angeles where colored folk didn't live. But at the hospital they were well represented in the kitchen, cafeteria, laundry and elsewhere. They were the workers who came from South Central L.A. to do the menial work at the hospital. And, like me, they were glad to have a job.

My duties were familiar—working the cafeteria line, waiting tables, working and helping in the kitchen. I quickly learned that even though my job paid only $2300.00 per year at the entry level and didn't go up much higher than that, it meant a lot in the credit market. There were workers, on my pay scale with two years on the job, who had mortgages and loans on automobiles. If a person had steady federal civil service employment, a GI Bill loan guarantee, and a low down payment, he was in a privileged position and had the tickets to a house, a car and more. My co-workers, with their striving for a middle-class life and a willingness to work hard for it, reminded me of colored folk in the Ville, in St. Louis.

In the summer of 1949, I borrowed money to buy a car, a 1935 Ford. And until I learned a different way to work, I followed the bus route along Wilshire Boulevard. We, my old car and I, were an unwelcome sight along the Boulevard, and the police made that clear. After tiring of police stops along Wilshire, I sped up my effort to learn another route to the hospital, finally taking the less glamorous Olympic Boulevard.

One sunny afternoon after work, one of my buddies at the hospital invited me to hang out with him and other co-workers at the beach. At the time, I didn't know anything about a beach in L.A., but I was game and said, "I'll follow you in my car." To my surprise, the hospital was only a few minutes away from the beach in Santa Monica. There, I got carried away with the amusement park and Municipal Pier that extended way out into the Pacific Ocean. It wasn't long afterwards that I began to stop at the beach almost daily after work.

My best friend, Nelson, an Army veteran from Louisiana, was out-going and well liked by everybody. Of average height, light brown-skinned, muscular and wiry at 155 pounds, he was a gifted Don Juan. Black and white women were attracted to him for his ability to say the right thing at the right time and in the right way. (I guessed his wife must have been an exception to the rule, for he was separated from her.) Nelson helped me settle in and learn the ropes at the hospital, treating me as a peer even though he was almost twice my age, at 35. In addition to a military background, we had a similar temperament—easy going and laid back—and we liked the blues, jazz, and Billy Holiday.

By the fall of 1949, things looked pretty good, having my own bedroom in a two bedroom apartment that Nelson and I rented in a nice neighborhood and having replaced my aged Ford with a 1947 Nash. Also, a tiny bit of Nelson's admirable ability to seduce the ladies rubbed off on me and made me a kind of junior-version Don Juan.

Credit in L.A. was a lot easier to get than the means to pay the bills, and I sometimes had trouble paying on time. When I mentioned the problem to Nelson, he said, "Take a couple of courses at my school, and the GI Bill will pay for them and give you $50.00 a month." So in January, 1950, I signed up for two—the minimum required in order to get a student stipend at Jefferson Adult Evening School. I registered for "Grammar & American Literature" and "Algebra I." It was in this integrated school in L.A. that I was finally ready to attend high school.

But, because of Agnes, whom I met through a friend of Nelson's who was attending Jefferson, it turned out to be a false start. We both enjoyed going to the amusement park and Municipal Pier at Santa Monica, spending so many evenings there and in my apartment that I missed too many classes. So once again I dropped out of high school without completing a single course.

Though he didn't change his basic lifestyle, a few months after I left my uncle's hotel for better digs, James did the same, landing in nice lodgings off

Central Avenue. Once while visiting him there, grinning with self-satisfaction, he told me he took the USAFI Tests of General Educational Development (High School Level) and scored high enough on them to get his high school equivalency diploma. I didn't know anything about the tests or an equivalent high school diploma before he told me about them. Much interested, I thought, "Hey, this is a good way to get a high school diploma without attending classes." So I asked him, "How do I go about taking them?"

He chuckled saying, "You haven't gone to high school yet. What makes you think you can score high enough on these tests? You need to take some courses first." And then to underscore the seriousness of his position and his contempt for the idea that I should even think about taking the tests, he dramatically announced the names of each test: "Correctness and Effectiveness of Expression; Interpretation of Reading Materials in the Social Studies; Interpretation of Reading Materials in the Natural Sciences; Interpretation of Literary Materials; and General Mathematical Ability."

I figured he was right, but having nothing to lose I decided to take the tests anyway. And so I went ahead with the application process, took the tests and forgot about them. A few months later, I received a notice from the Los Angeles City Board of Education Advisement Service informing me that my score on the tests made me eligible for a high school equivalency diploma and that I only needed to take a course in world history to get it. I had trouble believing it. And so did James.

One day Nelson was beside himself bitching about his wife from whom he'd been separated for several years. He said he worried that she was going to take him to court in an effort to gain partial ownership of some property he owned. Since he left her the furnished apartment and they had no children, he didn't owe her anything, he said. And to get beyond her reach, he talked about leaving California, saying he could easily transfer to another V.A. hospital in New York State. Curious, I asked, "Can you, really?"

"Yeah, Nakia would fix it up for me," he said.

"Who's Nakia?" I asked.

"She's a sweet little dietitian who transferred to some place in New York. She left the hospital before you came. On the QT, we had a thing going on. She'd be glad to get me there close to her," he said, not boastingly, but in a matter of fact manner. "Then why don't you write and ask her to fix you up with a job there, if you really want to leave California?" I asked.

He sounded as though he was serious and wanted badly to put some distance between him and his wife. So I pushed the idea of getting Nakia to help him.

"Maybe I will," he said. "And you could go with me. "You don't have any ties to L.A."

The idea of leaving L.A. had never entered my mind until then, and over the next few days it stayed there. It was true that L.A. never moved me like San Francisco or New York City, and it was largely for sentimental reasons that I returned. So the thought of leaving for New York State was beginning to look like a good idea.

In the spring of 1950, I wrote to Nakia asking about job opportunities at her hospital for Nelson and me. She answered right away, saying we could easily get the same jobs there as we had in Los Angeles. She also enclosed two application forms, telling us where to mail them. Her information about the V.A. Hospital being located in Montrose, a place up the Hudson River about forty miles from New York City, really pumped me up and caused me to imagine spending weekends in the Big Apple. I filled out my application and promptly mailed it off.

Excitedly, I brought Nelson up-to-date on what Nakia had written. But he didn't seem glad. I was mystified and asked him why he wasn't happy about her response. It turned out that since listening to him complain about the "heartless greedy bitch" his wife was, he discovered that she wasn't so bad after all. In fact, he said he was going to stop his womanizing and maybe go back to her. I didn't believe it; the truth was that he wasn't up to uprooting himself and seeking a new life way across the country. When I said I'd take the job if offered, he didn't believe me. "Why would you want to leave L.A.?" he asked, "You've got a nice car, an apartment, and Agnes. Why would you give all that up?" I said, "I would like to live in New York City, and being in Montrose would bring me very close to it."

With each passing day, Nelson continued to argue against me going to Montrose. Then one day I received a reply to my application, offering the same job and without any interruption in service and pay. That settled it, and I began making plans to go to New York. I had mixed feelings about leaving, but it was the right thing for me to do.

Although James and I hadn't seen a lot of each other, we stayed in touch. He was still doing his thing when I dropped by his place to tell him I was moving to Montrose. He received the news as if I'd said, "There's too much smog in L.A.," without a show of interest or emotion. But despite his apparent indifference, I had the feeling he was sorry to see me leave.

After selling my car, packing my things, saying goodbye to Nelson, Agnes, my uncles, aunts and everybody else, in July, 1950, I left Los Angeles for Montrose, New York via St. Louis where I planned a stopover for a few days to break up the long train ride and to visit Mama. I felt good about having a job I could transfer from one coast to another. The reaction of Mama and my brothers to the news of my being enroute to Montrose to live and work was—what is that boy going to do next?

I asked my brother Ben and his wife, Dot, if they could fix me up with a date so the four of us could go out together one night. They exceeded my expectations by getting me a date with a vivacious lady who was pretty, 5 feet 7 inches tall, 125 pounds, cafe au lait complexion, brown eyes, shoulder length brown hair and curvacious. Also, at 21 she was very bright, college educated and named Brunette. The family home, in which she still resided, was a large two-family house on a quiet well-kept street in the West End near the Ville.

Brunette knew I was born in St. Louis, yet she regarded me as a Californian on the way to New York. I liked that. We spent much time together in the waning hours of my stopover. On the morning my stay ended, she saw me off at Union Station.

16

Reunion

As the train began to move northeastward, memories of my first train ride in that direction came to mind. Then, I was on my way to boot camp in Maryland. This time, on my way to upstate New York, the ride was longer. It was many hours before the conductor called out, "Next stop, Montrose." When the train stopped, I pulled my footlocker up to the exit door, lifted it by its strap and slid it down the train steps to the ground. And before I could get my bearings, the train slowly pulled away. Looking in vain for another human being, I suddenly realized that there was nobody else around.

Struck by a feeling of utter desolation, I discovered there was not even a train station building or a railroad agent to assist passengers. I stood there alongside the train tracks with my footlocker resting on the dirt ground thinking, "The only reason to believe I am actually in Montrose is that the conductor called the stop," for there wasn't a sign anywhere announcing that this was it. Thanks to the conductor, I was comforted by the belief that I was where I was supposed to be.

Picking up my footlocker, I moved from the edge of the tracks to the side of a paved road. Suddenly a taxi came into sight. The driver pulled up, and I quickly got in with my footlocker. He said he knew of my train's arrival and decided to come by to see if anyone got off. On the way to the hospital, he gave a historical account of the area, explaining that the town owed its identity to the hospital. The entire area was now undergoing development because of it.

Shortly after I arrived at the administration wing of the hospital, an employee took me to the employees' domicile, a barracks like building complete with beds, lockers, showers and toilets. This was a spacious place with lots of room between individual beds and lockers. I was introduced to some of my co-workers, colored men ranging in ages from the 20 to 40 and from nearby Westchester and Rockland Counties. One of them asked me in apparent disbelief, "You left California to come here?"

Apart from the environment of Montrose, there was little that was new to me at the hospital. My co-workers, my duties as a food service worker and the hospital culture were all familiar.

One day shortly after settling into the routines, I overheard a cook call out, "Nakia," to one of the dietitians. Thinking it was the Nakia who helped me, I slowly walked over in her direction to introduce myself and thank her. But when she and the cook suddenly moved to another spot in the kitchen, I went back to my pots and pans without giving my thank-you speech.

After a few weeks, I'd made a couple of buddies. One guy, Bob, lived in Ossining, a Hudson River town. I told him I wanted to go there some day and see Sing Sing State Prison. He laughed when I asked him if he'd ever seen it, saying he passes it everytime he walks to the train station. I grew up on gangster movies set in New York City and heard a lot about Sing Sing and the bad guys who were "sent up the river," I said.

Tarrytown was another place I wanted to see. Bob was surprised to hear me mention this small village and asked why I wanted to go there. Having read "The Legend of Sleepy Hollow" and "Rip Van Winkle" and thinking they were set in and around Tarrytown, I wanted to go there, I explained.

"Yeah, you're right," he said, "I read those stories too." He said its easy to get to Ossining and Tarrytown; both places are down the road about 15 or 20 miles from Montrose. He said, "I'll take you there when I get my car out of the shop."

Bob was true to his word. One weekend, he drove me down to Ossining to see Sing Sing. Since I wasn't interested in touring the inside of the prison or seeing it up close, he slowly drove by it, giving me a chance to see its great walls and main entrance. What I saw of it wasn't as scary and creepy as I thought it would be. But enough. Bob said people in town were used to seeing it and didn't pay it much attention except when electrocutions caused temporary power outages in town.

I said to Irma, Bob's sister who joined us on the short drive down to Tarrytown, "Boy, what a different place from what I expected!" It was a far cry from the village in the Washington Irving stories. There was nothing sleepy about this little manufacturing town. And the horsepower in the cars assembled at its General Motors plant must have been the envy of the "Headless Horseman".

Brunette and I had corresponded with each other almost daily, since coming to Montrose in July. As the weeks passed, our letters increasingly became words from the heart, making it clear that we were developing a very special relationship. I enjoyed very much the feeling that someone as lovely as she cared about me. Yet it was not a "saving all my love for you" thing, for either of us. She hadn't declared me to be the only man in her life, and I still enjoyed the company of other women.

Being accustomed to Montrose and environs, I was eager to check out New York City. One night I called my Uncle James, Mama's brother who lived in Harlem, telling him I'd called before way back in 1946 and missed him. He explained that he worked on the road as a Pullman porter and was often away from home. He said he was glad to hear from me and suggested a time to come and catch him in town. I took him up on the date and time and went down to see him on a train which conveniently stopped at the 125th. Street Station in Harlem.

Uncle James, or Jimmy, as he preferred to be called, was a 46 year-old slightly built welterweight dynamo. He completed correspondence courses in air conditioning and refrigeration and then opened and operated a shop to repair refrigerator and air conditioning units. While all this was going on, he was still working as a Pullman porter, running between Chicago and New York City, without missing any time on the job.

Jimmy told me to think of his apartment as my home whenever I was in town. Saying Lottie, his wife, sometimes stayed overnight with friends when he was out of town, he gave me a key to the apartment. During the early days of autumn, 1950, I often went to New York City, spending much time getting to know Central Harlem. My streets of dreams were 125th. Street and 7th. Avenue. The fabulous Apollo Theater and the hip Baby Grand were on 125th. Street. Sugar Ray Robinson's bar, the Theresa Hotel, Smalls Paradise, and Flash Inn were on 7th. Avenue.

While sitting around my quarters in Montrose, on a day off, I began a serious effort to find out what happened to the Ole Man and Babe, by writing to the Ole Man's brother Gilbert in Oxford, Mississippi. To my surprise and delight, his wife, Aunt Fats, replied promptly in an upbeat letter, saying she was in touch with Babe and the Ole Man and gave me their telephone number and address in Cleveland. I called Cleveland right away and spoke to each of them. We were overjoyed hearing each other's voices and wept as we talked. I promised to come to see them as soon as I could.

Brunette and I kept up our letter exchange. In my letters to her, I talked about the isolation of Montrose, Jimmy and New York City and how I missed her. By October, I'd become obsessed with the desire to be with her and knew I'd have to return to St. Louis for that. So after 4 months at Montrose, I quit my job with the intention of going to St. Louis to spend some serious time with Brunette.

The night before leaving for St. Louis, I spent a lot of time talking to Jimmy in his apartment. I told him about Brunette, going to St. Louis, and my plan to return to New York City. He wanted me to consider going to a trade school in New York to learn a trade useful in helping him operate his business. Though I wasn't excited about the idea, I decided to give it a try. So before leaving for St. Louis, I applied to New York Trade School and was accepted in a 2 year, full time program under the GI Bill, with classes scheduled to start on February 5, 1951.

The day before leaving for St. Louis, I spoke of the Ole Man with Jimmy. I told him the story about the Ole Man's disappearance in St. Louis and that I was stopping in Cleveland to see him. He said he hadn't seen the Ole Man in many years and wondered how he was doing. They met, as teenagers, while each was working at a fraternity house on the campus of the University of Mississippi in Oxford, he said. The Ole Man worked as a waiter, and his job—as he laughingly recalled—was "swatting flies." Jimmy said the Ole Man was one of the smartest guys he knew, and when he learned that his sister, Mama, was going to marry him, he thought she was lucky, or as Jimmy put it, "She did good to get him." He also said, after I mentioned having heard some relatives badmouth him, "No matter what anybody says about him, he's still your father." He didn't comment on my reason for going to St. Louis, but he wished me luck and said I was welcome to stay with him and Lottie on my return.

The Chicago-bound train pulled out of Grand Central Station in New York, with me headed for St. Louis by way of a stopover in Cleveland. After a few hours underway, Jimmy came from the Pullman section of the train looking for me in the parlor section, as he told me he'd do if he had a chance. It was fun meeting him this way and seeing him in his Pullman Porter's uniform. We chatted for a few minutes, and he sent regards to the Ole Man.

From the train station in Cleveland, I took a taxi to the Ole Man's and Babe's. As the taxi drew nearer to the address, it wasn't long before the scenery took on a very familiar appearance. I thought to myself, "Oh shit, they're no better off than when I saw them three years ago." I left the taxi and approached the house, opened the gate of the swaying chained-linked fence, climbed the steps, and knocked on the front door. A middle-aged, scraggly black man opened the door. I told him the Ole Man's name and asked if he lived there. The man said he didn't know the Ole Man by name, but he thought the man I was looking for lived downstairs. I thanked him and made my way down the steps into the basement. Babe answered the door. Tearfully we hugged and kissed. Pointing to a bed in the corner of the room and with a look of utter despair on her face, she said, "There's yo daddy over there." I looked and saw him stretched out on the bed, drunk. Although I had seen him like that countless times in the past, this time I had absolutely no sympathy for him.

Babe and I ignored him and sat down at the kitchen table to talk. Babe was always a super housekeeper, and the little basement apartment was neat and clean. I asked her why they left St. Louis. She said, "Baby, he owed too much money. He drank on credit and owed some crooks who said they were gonna kill him if he didn't pay. So when my sister here in Cleveland told me to come and live with her, we packed what we could and took a bus here without looking back."

After hearing that story, I loved Babe more than ever, and I had to wonder why she put up with the Ole Man. After all, she was hard working, attractive and only 34 years old. She could easily have a better life by merely walking away.

For the first time in my life, I was angry and ashamed of the Ole Man. I walked over to his bed, shook him, and looked him in the eye to tell him what I thought of him. But I saw in his eyes that he didn't know what was going on. "Join AA," I yelled to him in disgust, as he sank further into the bed.

Babe and I cut through the gloom by recalling some happy times. I told her about Brunette and mentioned the possibility of marriage. Babe said she was happy for me and hoped things turned out the way I wanted. After much conversation and lunch, I returned to the train station and waited to board a train to St. Louis.

17

Great Expectations

When my train arrived in St. Louis, I went straight to Mama's apartment. She knew I was coming, but she didn't know why. She said, "I sure am having trouble keeping up with you." As much as I wanted to share my feelings for Brunette with Mama, I decided against it, for fear of having to listen to something disapproving. So I merely said that I quit the job in Montrose and was going to get another one at the V.A. Hospital in nearby Jefferson Barracks. Gradually, she learned what was really happening.

At the first opportunity, I called Brunette. And in the hush of Mama's living room, we talked for hours, saying how much we missed each other and how happy we felt being able to see one another again. Our marathon telephone conversation, filling me with joy and gladness, made me feel certain about what I was going to do. The following week, I proposed marriage. And without any hesitation she said yes.

After Brunette agreed to marry me, I figured what was left to do was simple: get the marriage license, find a preacher to marry us and then leave for New York.

Brunette, however, insisted on observing some formalities which, in my haste to return to New York, hadn't occurred to me. She wanted me to ask her brother Taft (her dad was deceased) for her hand in marriage and then formally announce our engagement. Besides that, she wanted to plan a simple wedding ceremony to take place in the family home with her minister presiding and a reception to follow. While all of this was not what I had in mind, I saw no problem with it and happily went along with her wishes.

Brunette, a twin and one of eight siblings, lived in a large two-family house owned by Taft, her oldest brother. He and his family occupied the second floor, while Brunette, two brothers and her mother lived on the first floor.

Her widowed mother, whose advice was sought on various issues, was beloved and respected by her family, relatives and friends. Like Mama, she had led her family from Mississippi to St. Louis in search of a better life. In our many conversations, she once told me she wanted her children to seek spiritual salvation in the Pentecostal church and to work hard in order to get ahead. She said the way to get ahead was not only to work hard but to stay put on the job and build up seniority. Mama Prince, as I called her, and Taft were the nominal heads of the family in which the ages ranged from 21 to 50 among the siblings.

Mama Prince, Taft and other siblings were aware that I didn't share their thinking about how to get ahead. They knew I was working at the V.A. Hospital in Jefferson Barracks and that this was my third job in three different states over the past six months. So much for staying put. While some of them wondered about me and saw me as an oddball, there were a few who reserved judgment and were excited about the prospect of visiting Brunette and me in New York City. Also, when they learned that I was going to a trade school to study electricity and electronics under the GI Bill on my return to New York, they awarded me a few B.T. Washington points.

Mama and Brunette got along well, but Mama didn't think I was ready for marriage. She thought I should wait until I had a job and a place of my own. Her attitude was predictable. When she said, "If you go through with it, don't expect me to have anything to do with it." I knew where she was coming from, but I respectfully went ahead with my plan.

At age 19, in January, 1951, Brunette and I were married in Taft's living room. My brother, Ben, was my best man and Brunette's maid of honor was her twin sister, Suenett. Our marriage was my second great adventure, and I was determined to make it work.

Our wedding reception was a joyful occasion and an opportuniy to meet many of Brunette's friends from high school, college and her workplace. I discovered how well regarded and extremely popular she was. Most of the guests were from the Ville and included a few guys who would have loved to have been in my shoes.

I telephoned Jimmy to tell him I had married and to ask him if he could put us up. He assured me he could, and it would be no problem. "Lottie would be happy to share the apartment," he said, "So don't worry about a thing." He reminded me that the apartment was often empty because he was on the road and during that time Lottie stayed with friends. Furthermore, he said, they were scheduled to move into a new apartment in a few weeks, and, because of us he'd get a two-bedroom apartment.

Because Brunette wanted to give her employer 30-days notice of her intent to resign, and since I wanted to register at the trade school in person, I returned to New York alone, leaving Brunette to join me later.

I arrived at Jimmy's apartment, located in the Harlem River Houses at 153rd.Street and 7th. Avenue, on the morning of January 15. His apartment was in a federally subsidized housing project, built in 1937 and meant to serve as a model for local governments. It included a nursery school, a community playground and an esplanade along the Harlem River, from which one could see Yankee Stadium across the river in the Bronx.

The project also included Rucker Park, which—many years later—became known as the summer venue for exciting basketball. There, a few visiting N.B.A. players and some local players—who put on quite a show—played. Sometimes the locals gave the N.B.A. guys all they could handle.

Also, 2 blocks down 7th. Avenue, were the upscale Dunbar Apartments—once the home of Matthew Henson, the black man who accompanied Admiral Peary to the North Pole. Two fashionable restaurants and a boutique or two were also nearby on the Avenue.

Confident that the pleasant environment of Jimmy's apartment would quickly dispel any uneasiness Brunette might feel about living in Harlem, I could hardly wait for her to join me.

Epilogue

In 1967, on a regular visit to Cleveland to see Babe and the Ole Man, Babe told me, with resignation in her voice, "Baby, your daddy's heart is in bad shape. You know he had another attack since you were here." She was deeply worried, recounting how she drove through the streets speeding and running red lights to get him to the hospital.

The Ole Man was troubled too. And having things to do, he was a man in a hurry. "I filed for a divorce from your mother," he said, "and I'm going to marry Babe. It's the right thing to do."

His marriage to Babe, in 1968, was a crowning achievement on the road to redemption, he said. Marked atonement started in 1958, when he became an active member of Alcoholics Anonymous and began to help many others afflicted with the disease. Later, as a member of his church's Board of Trustee, he obtained funding for the creation of a day care center to help the church's working mothers.

His employment at Carlings Brewery—from which he retired as a maintenance worker and a part-time bartender—was a severe test of his resolve to live free of the influence of alcohol. "Once he started with AA back in 1958, he stopped drinking, and ever since then, he never drank more'n a beer every now and then," said Babe, with pride.

In February, 1970, at age 66, time ran out. A third attack took his life, catching him still in the act of trying to make amends.

After the funeral, when my brothers and members of their families had left to return home and Brunette and I were preparing to leave, Babe said to me, "Baby I don't know what I'm going to do without him." I wanted so much to say something comforting, but I couldn't think of anything. So I hugged her and said we'd keep in close contact, encouraging her to call us at anytime and to reverse the charges.

For more than a year, she suffered from depression but got through it. Soon afterwards, she married again. And more than once during that marriage of more than 20 years, she'd say to me, "Baby, I sure miss your daddy." Surviving her husband, Babe passed away in March, 1994, at age 77. We were in close touch til the end. Speaking to me early one morning from her hospital bed by telephone, she said, "Baby I'm real sick." In less than an hour later, she was gone. And, as she requested, I made arrangements for her funeral and burial. Her body was laid to rest in the same cemetery as that of the Ole Man's.

Mama, having sons living in New York City, Indianapolis, St. Louis, and Los Angeles got around quite a bit over the years, helping to care for her grandchildren—and in my childless case, helping Brunette with housekeeping and cooking chores. In her advanced years, exercising her independence, she lived alone. Being frugal, she managed to save a little money, and with her social security benefits, she met her financial needs. Ben helped her obtain an apartment close to him in a community near Phoenix. On my last trip out there to visit her, we sat together on her sofa talking, as we had become accustomed to doing. "You stuck with me all the way," she said, with a loving tenderness that caused me to weep. Two months later, in November, 1996, she passed on, at age 91.

Instead of a career in music, James became a teacher of Spanish. He and his wife had two sons together. She passed several years ago, leaving him seriously affected. Today, he is retired and still living in Los Angeles.

After distinguished civil service careers, Joseph and Ben are also retired.

About The Author

George Hemingway Isom is a graduate of the City College of New York with degrees in history: B.A., 1965 and M.A., 1971. He earned an Ed.M. degree, 1972, in secondary school curriculum from Teachers College, Columbia University, and he holds a Ph.D., 1980, in educational administration from the University of Iowa. In the New York City Public School System, for ten years prior to his retirement in 1993, he taught English to gifted and talented 8th. grade students in Bedford Stuyvesant, Brooklyn; in 1968 he organized and taught a seminal course in African History to 8th. graders in the South Bronx; and for two years in the late 1970's he taught in the College of Education at the University of Iowa. He is listed in the 1990 edition of *Who's Who Among America's Teachers.* In 1973, as Program Manager in the Division For The Disadvantaged in the New York State Education Department, he established the extant Long Island regional office charged with allocating millions of dollars in Title 1 funding of supplementary educational programs for needy students in both Nassau and Suffolk counties on Long Island and in Westchester and Rockland Counties. As a staff member of the School Superintendent, District 7 New York City Public School System, he organized, developed and coordinated a district-wide program in African-American History and Culture, in 1969. In the late 1960's he served on the editorial board of Buckingham Learning Corporation for which he wrote and published: *Martin Luther King Jr.: Apostle of Nonviolence,* 1970 and *Marcus Garvey: Father of Black Nationalism,* 1971. He lives on Long Island with his wife, Jeanne, and his cat, Chloe.

0-595-33804-6

Printed in the United States
40481LVS00004B/54

9 780595 338047